T0286210

Starting a Spiritual Business:

Inspiration, Case Studies and Advice
Featuring Diana Cooper and Ian Lawman

Starting a Spiritual Business:

Inspiration, Case Studies and Advice
Featuring Diana Cooper and Ian Lawman

Charlotte Anne Edwards

BOOKS

Winchester, UK
Washington, USA

First published by O-Books, 2014
O-Books is an imprint of John Hunt Publishing Ltd., Laurel House, Station Approach,
Alresford, Hants, SO24 9JH, UK
office1@jhpbooks.net
www.johnhuntpublishing.com

For distributor details and how to order please visit the 'Ordering' section on our website.

Text copyright: Charlotte Anne Edwards 2013

ISBN: 978 1 78099 710 0

All rights reserved. Except for brief quotations in critical articles or reviews, no part of this
book may be reproduced in any manner without prior written permission from the publishers.

The rights of Charlotte Anne Edwards as author have been asserted in accordance with the
Copyright, Designs and Patents Act 1988.

A CIP catalogue record for this book is available from the British Library.

Design: Stuart Davies

Printed and bound by CPI Group (UK) Ltd, Croydon, CR0 4YY

We operate a distinctive and ethical publishing philosophy in all
areas of our business, from our global network of authors to
production and worldwide distribution.

CONTENTS

Acknowledgements

To Golnaz, my best friend, and Daniel, who has taught me so much.

"A shortcut to manifesting your desires is to see what you want as absolute fact"

The Secret

Preface

As Deputy Editor of a spiritual magazine I would receive countless emails from people asking me how they could leave their mundane 9 to 5 and start their own business in a more fulfilling, spiritual vocation such as Reiki.

I realized that these people had what it took to succeed already: a passion for their subject, a desire to heal others and the dedication and ambition required to excel. They just needed the confidence and encouragement to take the plunge—and that is what *Starting a Spiritual Business* aims to do. I've compiled real-life stories, practical advice and inspiration from talented healers and therapists from across the world who have made the transition from their 'normal' job to living their dream—perhaps they are now working as a Reiki practitioner, Angelic Healer, Crystal Healer, Psychic or Medium, Aromatherapist or Hypnotherapist.

I hope their stories will inspire you and give you the oomph to start your own brand-new chapter in life and take control of your destiny. At the end of the book you'll find practical and financial advice, as well as a directory of useful contacts. CE.

Foreword

by Alexandra Wenman, Editor of *Prediction magazine*

Most of us spiritual sorts are really great at putting others first. We make awesome healers and therapists, and brilliant counselors. But when it comes to the world of business and the practicalities behind setting up a practice, many of us just don't have a clue where to start.

Perhaps we picked up our financial failings from a past life—vows of poverty ringing any bells? Or maybe being in the limelight scares us half to death—witch trials, anyone?

Wherever you feel you need a little help in getting started with your spiritual business, you'll find the answer within these pages.

Packed chock-full of golden nuggets of advice and guidance, this book is like a deluxe chocolate box (raw, of course!) of top-notch information, and just about every flavor you can think of is on the menu!

Covering everything from how to choose the right course or credentials to suit you, to how to start out as a teacher, to practical and financial advice—and there's even a handy section on helpful contacts.

Charlotte Edwards is a true inspiration. After starting this book, she found herself battling severe depression, and bravely delved right into her own shadow, facing all her insecurities and issues until she finally pushed through to discover the light of her own dazzling spirit. The result is what I would like to call a 'work of heart'.

Much more than a practical guide, this book contains real stories of real people who made the bold step from student to sage... and succeeded. It is the ultimate savvy spiritualist's business bible.

At last, like Charlotte, we can step boldly out of our shadow and let our light shine... (and help even more people in the process—because that's what we do).

Chapter 1

A shift in consciousness

The human mind is like an umbrella; it functions best when it is open
Walter Gropius

It's 2013 and the earth is undergoing a massive, almost violent shift in consciousness, moving from a destructive and draining manner of existence to one that is based around acceptance, peace and sustainability—and it is happening at breakneck speed. For millennia we have been evolving and it finally seems that our 'survival of the fittest' instincts, which served us so well in the past, but have caused so much suffering in recent centuries through war and poverty, are fading. Many of us are recognizing that we can live life in consideration and harmony with each other, spurning our 'Selfish Gene', as coined by Richard Dawkins. We're realizing that things need to change—societies and individuals are experiencing a profound shift from a negative state to a positive one, and this transition isn't always pleasant. I for one spent six dark months battling severe depression before I finished this book. They were the most frightening months of my life, but they were also months that led me to emerge from the darkness almost immediately into the light, finding myself blessed with a new, more fulfilling direction in my career (I am a writer) and a greater sense of peace within.

I'd like to invite you to read the truly inspirational stories of people from across the globe who have embraced this shift in one of the most courageous and beautiful ways: following their dream to become a healer, and starting up their own healing business. I hope that you take motivation from these wonderful people and do the same yourself, and help to create the world that we, as divine and incredible beings, deserve to live in.

Many women work in healing professions, which is unsurprising since women have always been healers, using herbs, astrology and trance states among many other methods to cure their patients, and passing their knowledge down to their daughters. As psychologist Erich Neumann said, "From time immemorial woman, in her character of Shaman, sibyl, priestess and wise woman, has influenced mankind." Ancient Egyptian priestesses who served the goddess Isis were known for their healing skills. In Ancient Greece a woman named Agnodice risked death by disguising herself as a man to train in medicine, as this was forbidden for a woman. She eventually set up her own practice—previously many women had died because they didn't want to be seen by a male physician, so when they realized Agnodice was a woman they flocked to her, and the law on female physicians was changed. Before Christianity spread, Europe was pagan and herbal healers and so-called wise women were accepted and respected. Sadly, Christianity suppressed these traditional methods as the Church associated disease with demons, and believed them to be a punishment from God. Anyone who was educated in the art of medicine was therefore thought suspect. Disease was 'cured' by the clergy or by prayers to the saints—and medicine went backwards. Happily, many of us now recognize the benefit of alternative methods of healing.

Natural healers

Trotula of Salerno

Thought to be the first female professor of medicine, in the 11th century Trotula wrote many books on women's health. To guard against miscarriage, she recommends the physician to, "Take oil, wax, powder of frankincense and mastic and mix them, and let the woman be anointed in front and back two or three times a week. This very much strengthens the womb and the cotyledons."

Hildegard of Bingen

Healer and mystic Hildegard lived in the 11ᵗʰ century and, among many other achievements, wrote books on medicine. As well as practical advice on staying well, such as eating a good diet, she also used gems, plants, herbs and tinctures in her work.

Elizabeth Blackwell

Born in the early 18ᵗʰ century, Elizabeth was a physician and studied botany; she wrote *A Curious Herbal*, which was published in 1737 and included descriptions and images of plants, how to prepare them and which ailments to treat with them.

Edward Bach

Creator of the Bach Flower Remedies in the early 20ᵗʰ century, Edward was also a spiritual writer and physician.

Deepak Acharya

Born in 1975, Deepak is studying the herbal knowledge of the Dangs and Aravallis healers in India, and has also published a book on indigenous healing medicines, *Indigenous Herbal Medicines: Tribal Formulations and Traditional Herbal Practices.*

Healing success

At the end of the book you'll find lots of practical and financial advice on succeeding at your holistic business. You may also like to try these alternative methods:

- Try burning cinnamon essential oil for business success.
- Remember these words from *The Secret*: "You are the designer of your destiny. You are the author. You write the story. The pen is in your hand, and the outcome is whatever you choose."

- Repeat this affirmation by Louise Hay: "I love myself, therefore I work at a job that I truly enjoy doing, one that uses all my talents and abilities, working with and for people that I love and love me, and earning a good income."
- Try this spell from Judika Illes' book *The Encyclopedia of 5000 Spells*: "To break through business blockages, grind bay laurel leaves, cinnamon, frankincense, tonka beans and vetiver roots together. Burn the resulting powder, allowing the aroma to permeate all areas of business."
- Call upon Archangel Michael for support in following your life's purpose.

Moving forward

There is one universal goal that everyone on earth strives towards: happiness. But what is the best way of achieving it? For many of us, happiness comes from helping others. Some of the most inspirational stories of those who have found contentment are the tales of people, such as St. Francis of Assisi, who sacrificed their own comfort to help those less fortunate. Of course, for us mortals achieving a sense of contentment and inner peace in today's world isn't easy—we have jobs, relationships, mortgages and finances to manage and worry about, all of which are external factors but all of which can and do affect our moods and emotions. When everything is living up to our expectations and vision, we feel on top of the world. But if one cog breaks down—perhaps the love of our life ups and leaves with little warning or compassion—our entire world can come crashing down, and other areas of our life suffer.

It is an oft-quoted truth that we must look inside for happiness and love ourselves, while realizing and accepting that no person or external factor should be allowed to affect our capacity to feel content. This is easier said than done and we take a while to learn how to do it. But, if we want to start a career in healing and helping others, we really do need to start with 'the man (or woman!) in the mirror' and focus on loving and healing ourselves first.

So, do what makes you happy and what helps you to love yourself. If you're in an unfulfilling job or you feel that your calling lies elsewhere, take control of your destiny and start taking the steps required to move into a more spiritually fulfilling career—it's never too late for a clean slate. Go ahead and do it now! Mentally wipe your slate clean, get rid of baggage and negative or pessimistic thought patterns and take the reins; your life is yours and you can change it at any point you wish. At every stage of our lives we are given choices and forks in the road— take the bull by the horns and go down the path you really want to travel; after all, none of us know how much time we have left so why not seize the day and go for it? Retrain, reorganize and flow with the change.

Set your intention

Sri Mata Amritanandamayi Devi—or Amma, 'The Hugging Saint'—once spoke of her views on the language of the heart:

> Those who speak this language do not care about their ego. They have no interest in proving that they are right or that anyone else is wrong. They are deeply concerned about their fellow beings and wish to help, support and uplift others. They are the givers of tangible hope and of light in this world. Those who approach them are reborn.

People who enter healing professions such as Reiki, Crystal Therapy and Angelic Healing don't do it so that they can achieve material success or recognition. Rather, they embark on their chosen path to heal, love and to provide their clients with the power to achieve greater harmony and happiness in their lives. Keep similar intentions close to the heart of everything you do, and financial success and a good reputation will follow organically.

Getting to where you want to be in life will happen only if you believe it will and if you make practical moves to get there. That sounds obvious, but so often people dream about their ideal job, but that's all they do. You make your future every second of the day through your choices—do you stay in, visit friends, answer the phone or let it ring out? Each decision shapes the rest of your life in some way. Perhaps if you'd gone out, you'd have met someone who would end up changing your life. Taking your first step to switching professions can be as easy as enrolling in a part-time or distance learning course that can be fitted around your day-to-day life. "If you believe you can do a thing, or if you believe that you cannot, in either case you are right," said Henry Ford. Choose to have faith in yourself. Quietly focus on your aim, work steadily towards it without rushing or hassling yourself and you'll get there. Don't use your energy worrying about an outcome that hasn't even happened. If things don't work out the way you hoped, don't feel defeated. Think back and remember a time when you felt upset after something didn't go to plan. You'll likely recall that although you felt awful at the time, the setback led to something even better! This has certainly been the case for me. Embrace change and deviations—it's good for you.

Say 'yes'

Success is about attitude. My best attribute is my positivity; it's led me to achieve much of what I set out to do. Positivity at its simplest is telling yourself 'yes'. For example, one of my goals as a young woman was to move to London. I was £3,000 in debt, had no savings and had no job to go to—but I quit my job, found a friend who was willing to move with me and did it. I would only accept a job in journalism or as an editor as that was what I wanted to do. After three months of applications and interviews, I was offered a wonderful job, complete with one week's training in the US. If I'd have told myself 'no' when I thought about moving—using the excuse of having no money, no savings and no income—I'd have gone nowhere. Instead, I set my sights on my goal, and went for it. At no point did I contemplate the idea that it wouldn't work. I knew I'd do it, and after some hard grafting I made it.

If you feel fear, turn it into passion; if you feel anxiety, channel that stressful energy into a positive action to get rid of the cause of your anxiety rather than passively worrying. Be excited by your goal, not intimidated. By all means weigh up the pros and cons and carefully look at your options, but don't talk yourself out of it unnecessarily. Some things we have to leave to chance—you never know who or what might come your way to help you on your path. If you keep an optimistic attitude, things will start falling into place. When you think positively, you'll see things differently, perhaps spotting opportunities and meeting people you wouldn't have, had you nurtured a defeatist attitude.

Who are you?

Pinpoint your strengths and harness them to work towards your goal. If you're quiet and don't like public speaking, make use of your writing skills or use the Internet, email and social media as much as you can—maybe you can even write a book using your experiences. If you hate writing and feel more comfortable on the phone than texting or emailing, focus on making connections this way. I hate public speaking so I get my message across in written form. It works well for my personality and my skillset, and I enjoy it. As a teenager, I worked very hard to appear more confident and to disguise my shyness. Doing this was beneficial and helped me to grow, but I never tried to change my character. That's almost impossible to do—you can alter the way you interact and react to situations and people, but not the way you feel inside. Remember, although you want to make others happy, accept who they are and to heal them, you must likewise apply the same approach to the way you treat yourself.

Consider the way you work:

- Do you focus on one thing alone until it's done, working swiftly with great focus?
- Do you multitask like crazy, completing things simultaneously and working quickly but accurately?
- Do you plan ahead, organizing each detail in advance before beginning?
- Perhaps you stop and start, taking a break from your project when you hit a creative block, and then get back to it when you've got more ideas.
- Maybe you thrive on a deadline, leaving everything to the last minute.
- Consider how much you enjoy working with others — would you like to have a business partner? Or would you prefer working alone without outside input? Are there gaps in your knowledge that would make a business partner invaluable?

Understanding how you approach projects will allow you to tailor your strategy to your character.

In the chapters ahead, we will look at case studies from people who have built successful businesses in Reiki, Angelic Healing, Crystal Healing, Psychic and Mediumship work, Aromatherapy, Hypnotherapy and other healing therapies. Nearly all healing arts can be run from a home office and treatment room — or, you could hire a room in a clinic, or rent or buy a property. Working from home, however, gives you the chance to pick and choose your hours, perhaps sticking to part-time until you are established enough to give up your day job. With time and experience, many of these careers will allow you to move into teaching your chosen profession through workshops and talks, if you so wish.

Chapter 2

Alternative therapies

Here is an overview of the healing arts covered in this book — what they are, how they work, what you need to enter the profession and what the working conditions are like. I'm focusing on Reiki, Angelic Healing, Crystal Healing, Psychic and Mediumship work, Aromatherapy and Hypnotherapy, although many other alternative therapies are also covered at the end of the book in Chapter 10.

Reiki

What is it?

The purpose of Reiki is to heal: there is no religious belief attached to the practice. Reiki works with the universal life-force energy that flows through each person. Stress, illness, depression and other negative factors can cause blockages in this energy and it is the Reiki practitioner's job, through the placing of her hands on or just above specific areas of the body, to clear these stoppages with positive energy and get it flowing freely again. The client may lie down or sit — whichever is most comfortable. Following treatment, he or she should feel an increased sense of mental and spiritual peace, relaxation and harmony, and may also feel physically energized.

To become a Reiki practitioner, you need to become 'attuned'. As such, the practice isn't one that can be learned in the conventional sense; the skills must be transferred to you from another.

Could I do it?

Anyone can start training as a Reiki practitioner. There are three levels of proficiency:

- Level One
- Level Two
- Level Three—or Reiki Master

You'll need to have an empathetic and non-judgmental personality, be able to put your clients at ease and find out what their needs are and have the ability to forge long-lasting client relationships.

What are the working conditions?

- Many people work from home, with one room put aside as a treatment room. Each Reiki session will normally last up to an hour.
- Consultations and record-keeping are important, especially once you build up a book of repeat clients.
- Some distance healing may be involved.
- Self-promotion, marketing skills and advertising will be required.
- Those who become self-employed will need to learn bookkeeping skills.

Angelic Healing

What is it?

Light, love, purity and healing are the cornerstones of Angelic Healing. The Angelic Healer works with the Archangels, angels and other celestial beings by channeling their energy with the aim of using it to heal emotional, spiritual and physical ailments in their clients. Stress, depression and past life issues are some of the problems that can be addressed. Angelic Healing can be performed in person or via distance healing. Any negative energy held by the client should be dispelled following treatment, and he or she may feel an increased sense of peace following the session. It can be performed with the client lying down or sitting up and the practitioner does not need to know her client's reasons for seeking healing.

Could I do it?

People from all sorts of backgrounds move into Angelic Healing; all you need is a desire to heal. Many angel practitioners run Angelic Healing courses—but there are no official routes of entry into the profession, unlike Reiki, which has set levels of proficiency to study for and achieve.

What are the working conditions?

- Angelic Healers often work from home, dedicating a room to the purpose.
- Sessions last approximately one hour.
- Healing can be performed in person or remotely.
- Self-promotion, marketing skills and advertising will be required.
- Those who become self-employed will need to learn bookkeeping skills.

Crystal Healer

What is it?

Each crystal has its own unique vibration, and each of these vibrations has the power to positively affect certain areas in a person's energy field. Crystal Healers use the stones' vibrations to clear blockages in and balance their client's energy. Often, the color of the crystal will correspond to the chakra it is best used to work on. For example, jade and aventurine pair well with the heart chakra.

During a typical Crystal Healing session, which may last up to an hour, the therapist will place the stones on or around their client—who may be sitting or lying down—leaving the gems in situ for a certain amount of time. They may change the crystal's positions during the session, if necessary.

Could I do it?

- There are hundreds of crystals, and you'll need to be aware of the effects of each of them. People will come to you with a specific problem in mind and you'll need to be able to pick the most effective stones with which to work.
- Knowledge of the chakras and the body's Meridian lines is required.
- Crystal Healers may also advise on crystal use in the home, garden and workplace.

What are the working conditions?

- Crystal Healers could easily work from home, dedicating a room to the purpose.
- Self-promotion, marketing skills and advertising will be required.
- Those who become self-employed will need to learn bookkeeping skills.

Mediums and Psychics

What is it?

Mediums communicate with the spirits of the deceased, channeling their messages to the living—if appropriate. They differ from Psychics, who use extrasensory perception and telepathy to help their clients, access the Akashic records—a spiritual library of all that ever was and will be—and consult Spirit guides to offer counsel and advice. Mediums may choose to work with the media or lead ghost hunts, whereas Psychics may prefer to work one-on-one with clients—also an option for Mediums. Psychics and Mediums may receive information from the other side visually, or through sounds and emotions conveyed to them.

Could I do it?

Many Psychics and Mediums have had a connection with Spirit from a young age, and choose to enter the profession only once they've learned to control and work with their ability. If you don't feel that you've opened up your sixth sense, there are exercises you can follow to do so, as well as visualizations to cast protection around you as you work with spirits. There are plenty of developmental groups that you can join to help progress and strengthen your abilities.

Your desire to become a Medium or Psychic must be based upon a sincere and selfless wish to help and heal others—otherwise, you'll experience a very low success rate and exposure to negative spirits.

What are the working conditions?

- Psychics can work from home or rent rooms in commercial organizations—for example, the Psychic Sisters are based in a small curtained area in Selfridges, London.
- Mediums can use their talent to lead séances and ghost hunts, working with different people every week, and may also be based at home.
- There is the option for Psychics and Mediums to work in more lighthearted capacities, for example, doing psychic readings at fairs. You will come across more distrust of your abilities in these situations, so it's helpful to have a thick skin and an easygoing attitude toward skeptics.
- Self-promotion, marketing skills and advertising will be required.
- Those who become self-employed will need to learn bookkeeping skills.

Aromatherapy

What is it?

An Aromatherapist uses essential oils in a therapeutic manner to help positively affect their client's emotional, spiritual and physical state of well-being. The oils can be massaged onto the body—paying attention to acupressure and reflex points—inhaled, placed in bath water or added to lotions. Aromatherapy may aid conditions such as depression, stress, headaches and insomnia. Sessions can last up to two hours, and often more than one treatment will be recommended.

Could I do it?

- As well as excellent knowledge of essential oils and their properties, it is useful to have an understanding of human physiology and anatomy.
- Training in massage, acupressure and reflexology will be useful.
- You'll be conducting consultations with new clients, so good listening skills and an empathetic nature are important.
- You'll need to keep organized patient records.

What are the working conditions?

- Working from a home office and therapy room is a possibility, although you will likely need a large, suitable storage area in which to safely keep the oils.
- Self-promotion, marketing skills and advertising will be required.
- Those who become self-employed will need to learn bookkeeping skills.

Hypnotherapy

What is it?

A Hypnotherapist works by taking a client into a deep state of relaxation where they remain completely aware of what they are saying and are acutely focused on the hypnotist's voice. The hypnotist will then use questions and suggestions tailored to the client. For example, suggestive hypnotherapy will use suggestions to help a client break a destructive habit or provide them with confidence in a certain area of life, while analytical hypnotherapy will target the root of the issue rather than the symptoms. There is also the field of past life regression, between life regression and future life progression—the client may simply be interested to see what they find, or they may wish to release emotional blocks that are affecting their current incarnation. The emphasis throughout is on helping the person to change their life for the positive, allowing them to leave the session free from whatever negative emotions were troubling them.

Could I do it?

- You'll need the ability to build up a trusting and empathic relationship with your clients.
- Taking a counseling course will help with pre- and post-hypnosis discussions with your client.
- You should record your sessions so that the client can listen to them again at home.
- On days when you may not be feeling your best, you will still need to give your clients 100% of your energy and attention as you cannot take a coffee break during a session!
- Train with a reputable organization—a course in Neuro-Linguistic Programming (NLP) may also be useful.

What are the working conditions?

- Working from home is possible—although you will need to provide your clients with a comfy chair and a blanket to keep them warm during the session, and you'll need a space where you can be sure of no interruptions.
- You'll need recording equipment to document the session.
- Self-promotion, marketing skills and advertising will be required.
- Those who become self-employed will need to learn bookkeeping skills.

Chapter 3

Reiki

The five principles
Just for today, I will not be angry.
Just for today, I will not worry.
Just for today, I will be grateful.
Just for today, I will do my work honestly.
Just for today, I will be kind to every living thing.
Dr. Mikao Usui, founder of Reiki

Reiki clears negative energy from the client's energy field via the 'laying on' of the Reiki healer's hands. This can be via physically placing their hands on the client or by holding their hands slightly above their body. Treatment times usually range from 30 minutes to an hour and a half. This healing practice can help with stress reduction and relaxation; the recipient simply lies down or sits, fully clothed, and the healer places their hands in a sequence of positions around the body to carry out the healing, clearing negativity from the subject's life-force energy. It is used to treat all sorts of issues to do with the mind, body and soul, and can be learned by anyone. There are two main branches of Reiki: Western and Japanese. The main difference between them is that in Western Reiki the healer follows a set placement of hands along the body's main energy points and lines—the Meridian lines and chakras—while the Japanese form is more intuitive.

Practitioners will often practice their art on themselves to balance and strengthen their energy, as well as using it to heal people or animals. There are three levels of attunement, where the skills are transferred to you from another—these are: Level One, Level Two and Reiki Master.

The five principles of Reiki, listed at the start of the chapter, are the precepts that underpin the spirit of the practice. They're intended to allow those who follow them to live by their teachings and meditate on them to live a more connected life. They are simple, but profound—following them allows you to focus on the present moment, the 'now'—a truly liberating experience that can help banish destructive thought patterns when we worry about what happened in the past or what might happen in the future.

Reiki case studies

Melanie Elliott

Melanie is a Reiki Master Teacher with the Complementary Therapy Association (CThA) and runs First and Second Reiki courses. As well as Reiki, she also offers Crystal Therapy, Energy Interference Patterning, relaxation and meditation and ear candling (tranquilbalance.co.uk; +0044 1603 713 334).

"I'm a '40-something' woman who is just starting to experience life as I feel it is meant to be. As a child I was encouraged to do well at the traditional academic subjects and achieved average results, which enabled me to get an office job. At the time, this was seen as a great achievement and one that could offer a job for life, together with the associated benefits of good prospects, a regular income and financial security. I ended up staying with the same company for more than 20 years.

Towards the latter half of that time I developed clinical depression and was forced to take many months' leave. Medication enabled me to return to work, but I never felt like 'me'; it felt as if I was being what everyone else expected me to be.

Eventually, I stumbled across the idea of complementary therapies and was drawn to Reiki. After learning how to work with Reiki, I began to feel more like myself again—it became very clear that I could not carry on pretending to be someone else each day at the office. I made the decision to leave and set up business on my own.

Taking the first steps

I started to offer treatments to friends and family in the evenings and at weekends. Initially, it was like a paying hobby. Word soon spread and I began to get more customers. I started to advertise in the local community and attended fairs and events where I could showcase the treatments I was able to offer.

It was difficult at first to be out there alone with no one to fall back on, and no one to answer my questions if I needed help. The realization that I was the only person who could make my business a success was a tough one to get to grips with. But the most difficult thing to overcome was dealing with other people's disbelief and total lack of understanding as to why I was going to give up a high powered, well-paid career to go out on my own and set up business as a complementary therapist.

A new direction

There is no denying that the changes involved were significant, challenging and often brought me to the brink of giving it all up. It was hard to be isolated and alone, with no one to ask how I was or to strike up an idle conversation with. The only person to blame when things didn't go according to plan was me, and the realization that I could no longer rely on a regular income brought more than its fair share of problems.

But, gradually I started to build up a new network of likeminded people; those that had been there and were able to offer words of encouragement and practical support. I undertook a business course offered by my local council and attended workshops on advertising and bookkeeping to help myself get to grips with the practical aspects of being self-employed.

As a result of the challenges I faced, I am now more resourceful and feel greater responsibility for my own actions, mindful of how I can impact on others. I am more well-rounded and can see situations from a different point of view.

Best of all, I am me.

I no longer have to put on an act or pretend to be someone else, which I now realize was extremely exhausting. I am the director of my own play, the driver on my own journey. I have the freedom to make choices."

Melanie's tips on moving into Reiki

- Study for a certified qualification.
- Join a local support and/or discussion group(s).
- Become affiliated to official Reiki organizations.
- Become a registered practitioner.
- Be realistic about your expectations, especially when starting out.
- Build up gradually.
- Realize you are your own advert, whether you're at work or otherwise: your customers are more likely to remain loyal to you if they feel a connection with you.
- Set up a stall at local Mind, Body, Spirit events.
- Advertise: if people don't know you're out there, they'll never find you.
- Don't be dissuaded by others' lack of support or understanding.
- If something isn't working, change it.
- Follow your intuition.

Alexandra Wenman

Alexandra is the Editor of the mind, body, spirit magazine, *Prediction*. She is also an Angelic Healer and a qualified Angelic Reiki Master, as well as an Advanced Theta Healing practitioner and a Rainbow Children teacher. Her experiences with the angels stem from childhood, and she's been working with them ever since. Having had Angelic Reiki with Alex for emotional healing, I can testify that she is truly excellent, and works with unconditional love (angelic-intervention.co.uk; alexandra@ angelic-intervention.co.uk).

"I grew up in a little town called Coffs Harbour in northern NSW, Australia, and came to the UK about 14 years ago. I always wanted to write for a living and used to write stories and poetry when I was at school. At the same time, I was always fascinated by angels. As a little Catholic girl, my mum would help me pray to the angels every night. As I got older, I became more aware that whenever I wrote poetry it seemed to come from somewhere else—as though it wasn't me who was writing it but some higher force. It was also something I couldn't force. But to this day, the best poems and prose pieces I ever wrote were the ones where I had tapped into this unseen help.

I started my writing career in TV and showbiz journalism, working for *Who Weekly* in Oz, and then moving on to *TV and Satellite Week, TV Easy* and *What's on TV* in the UK. I freelanced for a few years on titles such as *Marie Claire* and *InStyle* before landing a job as Senior Sub Editor at *NOW* magazine. I went on to become Food Editor and was also given the role of Celebrity Party Reporter. During this time, I had really begun my spiritual journey and had trained as a Theta Healer and Angelic Reiki Master Teacher, so I wanted my career to reflect my true nature and values.

Changing direction

One day, I literally put a call out to the angels and asked for a job on a mind, body, spirit magazine. Within one month, I was made Deputy Editor at *Prediction*. Things moved very fast and I was asked to re-launch the mag within weeks of starting and then, six months later, I was made Editor. Through *Prediction*, I have furthered my spiritual growth and expanded the magazine, so I like to think that *Prediction* and I help each other out. We are on a spiritual journey together.

When I decided to teach workshops in Angelic Reiki, things fell into place so easily. Again, it was like it had all been orchestrated by forces other than myself. The very first workshop I ever did in studying Angelic Reiki was with Jayn Lee Miller in London, and I knew without a doubt that I was going to teach it one day. I didn't even know what it was when I signed up for the course, but I just felt so drawn to it. It is literally one of the most beautiful, and deepest healing modalities I've ever experienced.

Juggling jobs

The most difficult thing for me is balancing two careers—one as a magazine editor and one as a holistic therapist and workshop facilitator (well, three careers if you count my children's books which are due to be published very soon!). But when you're working with energy and the angels on a daily basis, you find that if things are meant to work out, they will. I have very much learned to go with the flow and make sure that when I am feeling stressed or tired, I just have to listen to my inner self and take time out.

It's funny, but it's like I know I am being looked after. Sometimes I worry about whether I will have enough people to attend a workshop (you need at least four to attend an Angelic Reiki workshop to hold the energy) but somehow I always get the bookings. Even if it's one day before the workshop starts and I don't have enough people, someone will usually book at the last minute. That's how I know I am on the right path and I must be doing something right.

The power of love

I have always been almost too trusting of people and, without fail, give people the benefit of the doubt until they prove otherwise. I used to see this as a downfall, but now I think it is one of my greatest strengths. I am beginning to really understand the depth of my capacity for love and, rather than that

25

being a weakness, I feel it is a great source of power in the true sense of the word. It is through this that I have also learnt discernment and how to accept and work with my shadow side. I feel this is both a great personal and spiritual strength.

My dear friend Sarah Katz (soulworkslive.com) has been helping me to step into my power this year and, for my birthday, she bought me a beautiful painting of a pearl inside a seashell. It says: "Your essence is your wealth." I used to have a very hard time loving myself and I would give my power away all the time, but now I see that being able to love others deeply and openly comes from loving yourself first and foremost. I now know how to cherish myself and that is the greatest strength of all. When you love yourself, it is so much easier to love others and see them for what they truly are despite their quirks and foibles: they are, simply, love."

Alexandra's tips on moving into Angelic Reiki

- Follow your own guidance—if something resonates, go with it. If it doesn't, don't.
- Make sure you retain healthy boundaries. Stop when you need to, and push yourself when you must—but don't let others take you for granted.
- Make sure you value your work and charge what it's worth—and so you can cover your costs. It's very tempting to give places on workshops away for free, but there's a lot to be said for the energy of exchange as well.
- Love what you do and have fun with it.
- Make lists and set goals. The first thing I did when I qualified as an Angelic Reiki Master Teacher was simply to set a date for my first workshop. I still felt I had no idea what I was doing or how to do it, but once I set that date, everything came together and my first workshop was a resounding success!
- Stay on top of your paperwork. I was never very good at

this—I'm a typical Libran and it's all about organized chaos with me, but I always know where everything is. I need to get better with filing, as opposed to piling, but whatever system works for you, use it—as long as you understand it, no one else really needs to (apart from your accountant!).

Penny Wing

Penny runs her spiritual and holistic healing business from the Costa Brava in Spain. She is a Reiki Master and Angelic Reiki Master, and a Master Teacher with the Diana Cooper School, and also offers a range of other holistic therapies and counseling (pennywing.com).

"I have always been a people person, and for many years worked in various jobs such as retail, tourism and other service-related industries. I've always been interested in alternative treatments, but it was not until I reached my 40s, when I was made redundant, that I knew I had to take control of my own destiny in terms of my career.

When we moved abroad to live in Spain, I needed to find work, so I decided to train as an Aromatherapist and holistic therapist. I enrolled on a one-year course and worked in the field part-time. Soon enough, it seemed my life was all about massage and essential oils—but I loved it! It was a few months after we moved abroad that I found Reiki—or should I say Reiki found me? One of my clients offered me a free session, and I was curious to try it.

Discovering Reiki

During this first session, very early on, I felt someone touch my nose—and it was not my client! I was wide-awake and it was not a gentle touch; it felt as if someone was running a finger down my nose from the top to the tip. When I mentioned this to her, she ventured someone was trying to get my attention—and trust me, they did.

I knew then that I was meant to work with Reiki, for whatever reason that was. I became attuned for Level One, and, three months later, Level Two, from which point I began to work with clients. However, it wasn't until the following year when I became a Reiki Master that I seemed to really 'open up' spiritually—then door after door opened and I now teach others how to work with Reiki, angels, Ascended Masters and other enlightened energy beings.

A pathway to healing

When I look back at the work I used to do and what I do now, I can see that the years of working with people and 'being of service' in various jobs had, in fact, prepared me for the work that I currently do. It's just now I work more with energy rather than physical matter.

I do believe that if you are doing the work you are meant to do, your Spirit guides and other beings will help you at every opportunity—this was certainly the case for me. You also have to ask yourself why you wish to become a spiritual therapist. Ultimately, this path is about being of service to others. It is so important to genuinely care about people—but you are not there to rescue people; they need to do that themselves. You are there to guide, encourage, support and to allow others to feel totally safe and secure whilst they are with you. The majority of my clients and students have gone on to become friends, which is wonderful. I personally find it very easy to change from therapist to friend and then back again whilst maintaining integrity and professionalism—but it can be challenging.

Know yourself

For anyone wishing to change career and start to work with Reiki or any other type of energy work, you need to remember that it is vital to work on yourself first. It is not about being the 'perfect' person—it is about being aware of your strengths and weaknesses. Working on yourself is an ongoing process that takes time and effort, but you need to be prepared to do it or people will not come to you. How can you expect them to work on themselves if you are not prepared to do the same?

For me, being spiritual is about being genuine, honest and trying to live my life according to the Five Reiki Principles. With the support of Reiki, my guides and my angels I am starting to finally understand how I can raise my energy frequency to the 5th dimension to ultimately live a more peaceful and happy life, although I am not there yet!"

Alison McLean

Alison McLean is based in Boorowa, New South Wales, Australia. She is a Reiki teacher and practitioner, and a member of the Australian Reiki Connection and the Association of Australian Reiki Professionals. Alison offers lots of wonderful spiritual classes and workshops, including meditation, Japanese Reiki, Australian Bush Flower Essences and spiritual retreats (naturaltherapypages.com.au/connect/denju; alison_mclean12@ hotmail.com).

A creative childhood

"The natural environment was my playground as a child and I have often felt dissatisfied with what I felt were mediocre and mundane pursuits. It would have been far less stressful for my parents if I'd done well at school and followed a traditional career path, but instead I joined the wonderful creative world of dance, theatre and modelling. This professional path sustained my life force for many decades through all the ups and downs. During my 40s and 50s my dance genres transformed as I explored world dance and music with their deep spiritual, cultural backgrounds—eventually leading me to expand my concept of dance as a healing art.

Discovering Reiki

There were several reasons why I decided to learn Reiki, but the main one was the fact that it was a spiritual practice and experience which one could use for self-healing. To me, it followed on from my own understanding of dance, movement, music and art. It all came from the same source. I also had injuries both physical and emotional that I believed would be supported through learning hands-on healing. When I started out, I didn't consider for a moment that it held the potential as a career avenue.

The next step

While I continued to be active in the dance community I was also dedicated to my personal daily Reiki practice and spiritual progress. I followed up with a Level Two course and, a year later, my Master Level. It was another 12 months before I began teaching and practicing professionally, although I constantly used my skills with family, friends and our animals. It is through these early stages of my commitment and dedication that I observed the incredible outcomes, and my understanding of working with spiritual energy grew profoundly. If I can't see how it works within myself and my situation with those close to me, how can I understand and empathise with others without judgment creeping in?

Becoming a teacher

As the years passed and I felt a deeper connection to my practice, I also became aware of gaps in my understanding. Just as I had always researched my music and dance when teachers couldn't satisfy my yearning, I began to research Japanese spiritual practices from centuries ago. I found a teacher, Frans Stiene, who with his wife Bronwen have authentically researched and continued the classical Japanese art of Reiki through a lineage of Japanese teachers. My Master Level the second time around satisfied my hunger and gave me a complete spiritual practice to sustain me for life. I felt a new, grounded confidence about passing on the teachings.

Challenges

I believe my greatest setbacks were rooted in my ego and a lack of knowledge, especially about grounding techniques. When psychic energy is stimulated through energy work, a lack of grounding can leave one very scattered, even egocentric. This does not make for a stable foundation on which to build a spiritual business. In the beginning, Reiki was all about hands-on healing and psychic awareness rather than a pathway to enlightenment and discovering my true nature, that pool of pure energy inside me that had remained unspoiled since the dawn of time. The inability to be deeply honest with myself in the early days was probably my number-one setback.

I don't have a brilliant business mind, but a few of my personal strengths are self-discipline, self-motivation and having a creative mind. I would like to think that now, in my maturing years, the spiritual strengths I'm developing are a sense of humor, patience, humility and compassion."

Alison's tips on moving into Reiki

- Maintain your personal daily practice.
- Be very clear and focused about what your business is, and what it isn't.
- Do a regular inventory to check your own thoughts and motivation, as this will reflect back to your clients and students.
- Keep the business as simple as possible without the trappings of useless accessories.
- Refer a client or student on to a doctor, health care worker or another suitable organization if needs be.
- Make sure the teacher you learn Reiki from is a member of

a registered organization, so you will be able to register yourself after qualifying, and also be covered by insurance.

- Think carefully about what you charge. It is important to cover your financial needs, but remember that a spiritual practice needs to be accessible for all interested community members. This is really tricky with a professional Reiki practice. Be creative by offering 'specials' from time to time, and be flexible with any opportunities you offer so that all can benefit.

- However, one must be careful to avoid burnout: look after yourself first so that you can continue to bring light into the world.

- If you can share a premises with other well-being practitioners, this will not only keep costs down but will also place you in the flow and circulation of a larger community.

Real-life Reiki

"Working with our daughter, Sarah, and her horses has led to painful yet divine experiences involving the world of spirit. When you buy a horse you're not quite sure what you have inherited from the previous owners. We bought a horse for our Sarah, which she renamed Zeus. Before long, he came down with Paterson's Curse poisoning and was not expected to live.

Using lots of Reiki energy for Zeus' hands-on healing led to unbelievable synchronistic events, which we could only put down to Spirit. Angel energy was abundant around Zeus as it guided us through the steps of his recovery and brought amazing people across our path at exactly the right time and under the most bizarre circumstances. I was working on a dance piece at the time and the music was called *Whisper of Angels* by Amici. I'd also bought a tiny angel figure for Sarah on this particular afternoon and slipped it into my bag as I paid the bill at the newsagents. It was the angel of hope, because hope was what we desperately needed. That same night, Sarah and I drove through the rain looking for a community hall where people were gathering to discuss the toxic problem that was killing so many horses and to see what could be done to help. It was so wet and dark that I lost my way and ended up in unfamiliar territory way off the main road. I stopped the car and knocked on the door of the closest house. The man who answered knew nothing about the meeting but when he found out about our sick horse he invited us in and introduced himself as someone who used to work for one of Australia's most famous horse trainers. He believed he could help us. My mind began to spin. How could this be possible? Of all the streets to be lost; of all the doors I could have knocked on.

As we stepped inside his house and I shoved the car keys into my bag, my cold fingers fumbled over the long forgotten angel of hope from the newsagents. This man spent the next few hours with us discussing the problem and looking over the blood test results which Sarah fortunately still had in her pocket. He wrote out a special diet for Zeus and told us all the dos and don'ts. It was going to be a long haul but recovery was possible. We never found out this gentleman's name but always refer to him as 'the angel of hope'. When we finally arrived home I reached inside my handbag and found the tiny figure. Tearfully I placed the angel of hope in Sarah's hand. Nine months later Zeus took Sarah through her cross-country exam with flying colours. These few words I wrote in a journal as a reflection."

Joanne Falchi

Joanne practices in Queensland, Australia and has a part-time job as an Usui Reiki Master Practitioner, working intuitively (joannefalchiusuiReikimaster.blogspot.com; joannefalchi@gmail .com).

"My career background has been varied over the years, and includes office work, property management, retail banking, bookkeeping, receptionist and human resources and administration. Due to severe allergies and allopathic (mainstream) medicine being unable to help, I turned to natural medicine for assistance and became interested in natural and alternative treatments.

While undertaking study in natural medicine, I started working as a receptionist at a natural health clinic. Part of my job was to describe the different treatment types to potential clients. Not knowing what Reiki was, I was given a Reiki treatment by the clinic's teacher—I was hooked! I felt like I had found where I was meant to be in the world, as if I had found my path. It felt like I had been away for an extended period and had now come home. I was relaxed, at ease, comforted and nurtured all at once, and completely at home.

Moving into Reiki

I signed up with the health clinic's Reiki Master to learn Reiki Level One. This unleashed a need in me to find out even more, so I signed up for Level Two to allow me to become a Reiki practitioner so I could share Reiki with everyone. My wonderful teacher instilled in me her passion for the healing art, showing me how easy, fun and effective it is, and how it consumes (unobtrusively) and incorporates itself into every aspect of your life.

To finish my Level Two training, I had to complete practical exercises and treatments on people, animals and plants. Finding willing human participants to complete my homework was difficult at times, as Reiki is a modality that is still not well known or understood in Australia. The biggest setback is the lack of awareness in what it is and how it can assist people. This continues to be a challenge, but through education by blogs, book and magazine articles, personal advertising, Reiki awareness seminars, health and well-being expositions, by offering free treatments at community events, and participating in Reiki forums and Reiki associations, people are slowly becoming aware of what it is and how it can benefit them.

In Australia, another setback is that private health funds have stopped covering Reiki treatments. They say their clients don't want Reiki treatments as part of their coverage—but feedback from the clients disputes this claim. This is being addressed by wonderful organizations such as the Australian Reiki Connection Inc. (of whom I am a member) by collecting client signatures on petitions and presenting them to the relevant health funds to let them know what their members really want— Reiki coverage."

Joanne's tips on moving into Reiki

Self-development

- Train with a recognized Master or teacher—a list of these are usually available from your local Reiki organizations.
- Become a member of a recognized Reiki organization.
- Join a Reiki group or forum so you can benefit from others' experience and advice without the hard slog of going through it yourself.
- Get feedback from people you practice on as to how they have benefited from their Reiki session with you. If you find a recurring benefit, you have found your advertising point for your treatments. This will also give you ideas on areas or places to advertise. For example, if you work a lot on small children and babies and the feedback from parents is that they settle more easily and quickly, then you could advertise in mothers' groups, childcare centers, hospital birthing centres and nurseries.
- Practice, practice, practice to get experience. Get family and friends to present with difficult issues or feedback so you can become at ease with handling whatever crops up. Also attend Reiki share groups with other Reiki practitioners to gain experience and feedback on how to

improve your treatments.
- Volunteer at places such as hospices.
- Word of mouth referrals from family and friends are free, and more likely to produce paying clients than any other form of advertising.
- Move into your career at a pace that suits you, your family, lifestyle and finances.

Business tips

- Reiki is meant to be simple and easy to do. The basic equipment needed is a sturdy massage table (for lying-down treatments) and a comfortable stool or chair (for seated treatments). Ambient items such as soft lighting, music and scent can be added as funds permit.
- Professional indemnity insurance not only gives peace of mind to your clients, it shows your professionalism — as does being a member of a recognized Reiki organization.
- Keep up with the latest research via forums and your Reiki organization, and use this information to advertise and educate existing and potential clients.
- Check with your local government agencies such as the local council, government small business organizations and trade practice organizations to ensure you comply with all the government requirements for setting up your business.
- Monitor where your clients come from so you know what advertising works and doesn't work. This will ensure you're not wasting your time and money with campaigns that don't bring results.
- Never be afraid to ask for recommendations and referrals.
- Use your Reiki skills to get what you want. Self-treat on a daily basis to strengthen your Reiki and resolve any personal issues you have. Use distance healing to the future to reinforce to the universe how you want your

business to build and progress.

- Put a business plan on paper. Write down how you want your business to build and progress and give time frames to these items. Write down how you are going to go about achieving them in the required time frame.

- Review and update your business plan regularly (at least monthly) to see what progress you are making. If some items are not being achieved or you come upon setbacks, research how you can get around them or ask for help from forums. We live in a fast-paced and ever-changing world. Flexibility is key to survival. If something is not working for you don't be disheartened or afraid to change or modify it.

What is... Animal Reiki?

Animal Reiki

This is Reiki performed on animals to aid relaxation, reduce stress, help them recover following an injury or an abusive owner, calm animals with difficult behavior or even give them peace as they pass over.

Moving into Animal Reiki, by Amy at Silver Daisies

"When I turned 30, I decided to go about leaving the rat race and pursue my dream of working for myself, helping people and animals using healing and holistic therapy. I had completed my Reiki Master training during previous years at my own pace—a passion for healing had hit me. In 2009 I took a Reiki for Animals training course and in 2011 I set up my Silver Daisies business, which has gone from strength to strength in the past couple of years. I now teach Reiki and Animal Reiki classes to students who wish to pursue a similar career or even just want to offer healing and alternative therapies to their own animals. I had no savings when I set up my business; it was built purely on passion, determination and a whole lot of positive thinking. My best advice is to be the kind of therapist and person you would want to visit yourself. Show your passion and commitment, and over time, your reputation will do the marketing for you in the most part." (silverdaisychain.co.uk; +0044 7889 069545)

In conclusion

- Always learn Reiki from someone who is a member of a registered organization so that you can do the same once you've qualified and so you'll be able to get insurance cover.
- Self-treat daily to heal any personal issues you may have and to ground yourself so you can do the best job for your clients.
- Always ask for feedback from your clients—if over time you notice a recurring talent for healing a particular problem or type of person, you have found your unique selling point.
- Join groups and forums of like-minded people for support and inspiration.
- Take evening courses in bookkeeping and marketing.
- Follow your intuition.

Chapter 4

Angelic Healing

Angels

Angels are divine and advanced spiritual beings that guide, advise and protect us. Those who connect with them feel unconditional love emanating from them, and a greater sense of peace within themselves.

Nearly all cultures have stories of angelic beings—in fact, very few have doubted that they exist:

- Angels are God's messengers in Judaism, and the Archangel Michael is the protector of Israel.
- Gabriel appeared to Mary in the Bible to tell her that she would give birth to Jesus Christ.
- In Islam, angels are divine beings who cannot fall from grace, but instead are tasked with various responsibilities such as being Guardian Angels or controlling the rain.
- Archangel Gabriel dictated the Qur'an to Muhammad.
- The Ancient Egyptians believed that each person had a 'Ka'—a spiritual double that stays with them throughout their life, protecting them like a Guardian Angel.

Today, more and more people are becoming conscious of angels. Some choose to express this connection by creating beautiful angelic art, performing Angelic Healing or Angelic Reiki, or simply connecting with the divine beings in their own personal way.

Angels will always help us—we do, however, need to ask, as the angels respect our free will and will probably not interfere otherwise. The solution to our problem won't appear on the spot—it's more likely we will suddenly know just what to do, or if we thought we had no way out of a situation, we may suddenly see a door. Angels will show us a path and then it's up to you and me to walk down it. Rather than asking the angels for a specific outcome to a problem or situation, simply telling them our predicament and asking for their help is all we need to do.

Communication

Connecting with the angels is not difficult at all—simply sit somewhere quiet, close your eyes and try to clear your mind. Then, focus on asking your angels for help, or invite them into your life, and ask for their guidance and protection. Always conclude by thanking them from the bottom of your heart.

Archangels

Angels and Archangels are able to help us in every part of our lives. Here are just a few Archangels and their specialties:

Chamuel

Gratitude, compassion, emotional healing: Chamuel can help those with low self-esteem, heal damaged relationships and protect against negative thoughts, such as malice, from others.

Gabriel

Communication, clarity, inspiration, guidance: Gabriel can help those who work in communication, such as writers, actors, teachers and politicians.

Jophiel

Wisdom, understanding: this Archangel can help with inspiration, concentration and clearing negative emotions to help you to connect with your higher self.

Michael

Protection, faith, courage, motivation: Michael provides spiritual, emotional and physical protection, as well as helping those struggling with commitment and dedication to their life path.

Raphael

Healing: for those who need healing, and those who are healers; he offers courage and guidance to help illuminate the way for those in emotional, spiritual or physical pain.

Uriel

Peace, compassion, spiritual service, creative expression: Uriel can also help people to stay strong in the face of negative events or thoughts.

Zadkiel

Forgiveness, tolerance, transformation: this Archangel can bring more joy to the world by helping people release negative thoughts.

Angelic Healers apply their craft in person and via distance healing, sometimes using email or the phone as well as face-to-face appointments to channel the angels and offer guidance. Many also offer courses and workshops as well as online courses, and some produce their own angel cards. The following successful businesses are all run by people who have a passion to heal others with the assistance of the angelic realm.

Angelic Healer case studies

Diana Cooper

Highly respected and world-renowned, Diana Cooper has penned countless wonderful, informative books on spiritual topics such as Ascended Masters, angels, and Archangels, elementals and unicorns. She also runs certified courses in angels, ascension, Atlantis and more—as well as courses to aid personal connection and study (dianacooper.com; scott@diana-cooper.com).

Diana's journey into Angelic Healing began after her divorce, which left her at rock bottom. Here, she shares her story:

"I had been an expatriate housewife for most of my 20-year marriage, and had not worked. My children were away at school and I had no skills. I was certainly bored. More important, I was terrified of living alone and had no idea how to earn a living. But, I did have a great wish to heal and help others—although at that point I had no idea that I really needed to heal myself. Despite having no spiritual or religious background, I called out to the universe for help and an angel came in and showed me my future as a spiritual teacher. This was the start of a very long journey.

I started out by training to become a Hypnotherapist and a healer. First, I needed to earn the money to train, and so had to do very basic jobs as I had neither the confidence nor the skills to do anything else. At this point I was still living in the marital home with my ex-husband, but had no access to money until I started divorce proceedings. Although I did not realize it, this was a very strengthening process. I gained in experience and learnt a huge amount. I kept notes of interesting experiences and case studies and used these when I started to write books. I walked a very narrow path and let nothing deflect me. I stayed open to the guidance of angels, and when the time was right I started the Diana Cooper School to train teachers to spread the wisdom of the angels.

My biggest hurdle was my fear that I would fail. However, on the opposite side of this was an iron determination to succeed—and this was greater. In the early days I often thought I would have to augment my income with a part-time job to make ends meet, but something always happened to change my mind. When I did not have enough clients I went out to market my work and envisioned many coming to me. Later, I had a waiting list and was more in danger of burnout!

My personal strengths are determination, compassion and a desire to make a difference. I also think self-examination and the humility to look at myself constantly are important. My spiritual strengths are faith, angelic connection and vision.

An angelic experience

Recently I was very upset by a hurtful comment. It was playing on my mind and I knew it was holding me down in the third dimension but somehow it kept churning. I decided to go into nature and ask the elementals and angels to take it from me. In the forest I stood in a clearing and asked them to lift the negative energy. In response I felt the elementals coming near to me. Then they started to sing my name. The angels then joined them, all singing my name, D—i—a—n—a, over and over again with great love. I could feel my heart chakra becoming hot and when I left the forest I could not even remember what the problem was.

The crown chakra and angels

Recently the angels have been expanding my crown chakra, and the journey for me has alternated between bliss and agony. It started when I was guided to ask the angels to touch the thousand petals of my crown: I visualized 1,000 angels in tiers of circles above me all stroking open the petals. That felt wonderful.

The following day as I walked with my dog I remembered how, when we stayed at Amma's ashram in Kerala, we would get up very early to hear the swamis singing the thousand names of God in their deep chocolate voices. It lasted more than an hour and was pure bliss. As I thought of this, the thousand petals turned into tier upon tier of angels above my head and I mentally asked them to sing the thousand names of God. To my astonishment, the angels did not sing the names one at a time but all together. It felt like a sonic boom into my crown chakra that they repeated seven times. I was nearly knocked out! So, the next day I tuned into my crown chakra and visualized the thousand petals opening. This time the angels asked me to 'om' and I did so. They sang with me—oh wow! The downside was that I woke in the middle of each night feeling as if my head had been cleft open with an axe and sick in my solar plexus—clearly higher energy being put through me. I had to lie there breathing into it, and this lasted into the day."

Opening up

This exercise will open your crown chakra, allowing higher frequency energy to enter you:

1 Find a place where you can be quiet and undisturbed.
2 Ask Archangel Michael to put his deep blue cloak of protection over you.
3 Ground yourself by visualizing roots going into the earth.
4 Call in Archangel Jophiel, the angel of wisdom, who is in charge of the crown chakra.
5 Ask him to touch your crown centre and sense or see all the 1,000 petals opening.
6 Be aware of 1,000 angels above your crown, forming tier upon tier above you.
7 Sense them stroking the 1,000 petals.
8 Ask them to sing over you.
9 When you have finished, relax and thank the angels before you open your eyes.

Diana's tips on moving into Angelic Healing

- Remember that the first step is just that—one step in the right direction, so choose a course that interests you, knowing that you will expand this as you gain in experience. Train somewhere solid like the Diana Cooper School, where you will be certified and be able to get insurance.
- Talk to everyone about your work. Your charisma will

attract clients to you.

- Set your boundaries and be clear about them. People will respect this.
- Once you have decided you are working with the angels, stick to your decision and they will support you. If you are doing spiritual work people expect you to radiate light, so relax and take time for yourself. This will ultimately benefit your business.
- Value yourself. You are doing important and valuable work, so charge accordingly.
- Spread your business cards and leaflets everywhere.
- Give talks wherever you can to get yourself known.
- Don't stick to one to one type of work—expand into groups and workshops as soon as you can.
- Write articles and get them out there.

Ros Place

Ros runs Angels with Ros. She offers online home-study lightworking angels courses, as well as those held onsite in London and Devon, UK. Her Course Leader Training course is aimed at people wishing to start their own 'lightworking with angels' groups and courses, or at those who wish to move into an angel-orientated career. Ros also offers downloadable visualization MP3s. She lives with her husband and two children in Devon (angels-with-ros.com; +0044 1392 580 744).

"Many clients and friends now call me the 'Angel Lady', which makes me feel very lucky and honoured. Every day I work with angels and Archangels who lovingly guide and support people through their problems and challenges. The angels will give you all of the guidance, information and advice you need in order to start 'creating' the life you really want. They are empowering and liberating. I love everything I do with the angels, from readings and healing with the Archangels, to spiritual development with someone's Guardian Angel, to all of the angels courses I run.

My professional background, however, is actually in insurance. I had worked in insurance and then cost drafting since I left school. I had only GCSEs; I tried Sixth Form and then college, but neither turned out to be successful academic experiences, although they were real fun! Strangely, I was always interested in teaching, as I felt that my personal school experience gave me a real understanding of how it feels *not* to understand. I tried at various points in my life to get onto access courses, but there seemed to be blocks all the way. Now I know why!

Knowing how it feels not to understand and having experienced learning difficulties really helps you to help others. The angels have now helped me to understand and learn easily by clearing my personal blocks and the limiting beliefs I held about myself. This was when everything changed for me.

Seeking my attention

I've always had a strong connection with the angels. I knew that they were there, heard what they were trying to tell me and for many years completely ignored it. I just wanted to be normal and fit in. So, for years and years I did nothing about it—until I reached 31. In this year my eldest son was born and my husband Eddie and I started to read about channelling. Really, it was he who was interested, and I was quite indifferent to it. Eddie always had loads of questions he wanted answers to, whereas I never did—I never really wanted to 'know' anything.

After a time, I started being woken up in the middle of the night by a very loving energy trying to move my jaw and breathe with me. It was as though the energy was working out how a physical body worked and how they could speak through me! It was really exciting, but I was just exhausted by it all. Zed, my son, was just a few months old, and I needed all the sleep I could get. This is when I learnt about boundaries—both in regards to the personal and spiritual life.

I moved into a more spiritual existence when we came back from travelling around Europe in our caravan. It had not been a spiritual journey at all, but a very revealing personal one, and I felt somehow I was ready to start doing what I knew I have come to earth to do. Despite this, there were still plenty of excuses or reasons why I shouldn't: for example, Eddie was working on a project that 'had' to succeed so that we could start to earn some money—the angels just kept telling me not to worry about Eddie's work and to get on with what I was supposed to do.

So, I did. It began with a conversation with someone who was having a difficult time and I heard myself telling him that the angels could help him. He asked how, and I told him that he could come to my house for their guidance if he wished. He did, and was as stunned as I was when his father, in Spirit, gave me some messages. So very gently, word got around locally that there was an 'Angel Lady' in the village, and people came to my front room to hear what the angels had to say.

Angelic career

Over time, I thought about teaching again. I started to run angel evening classes locally, which I loved, and began to generate more and more business this way. Then I got a website constructed and began to work with international clients over the phone or on Skype.

So far, there have been no setbacks as such—but it has been hard work to get to where I am. The work has been enjoyable and fulfilling, but when you're establishing yourself and you have two children as well, you need to be very focused and also very determined. The hard work has been powerful because it has shown me how much I want the path I have chosen. The angels tell me that there is a Success Guardian whose job it is to ensure your success retains its value. The Guardian will give you lots of chances to bail out, but these are just opportunities to develop a part of yourself.

Personally, I believe in having a strong passion; we should all strive to do something we believe in. As a teacher, I also think it is important to convey information in a clear and understandable manner, and in a way people can benefit from."

Ros' tips on moving into Angelic Healing:

- Don't do something you think everybody wants—do what you believe in and love.
- Don't put pressure on your spiritual work by giving up your other profession too soon. You can do both for a while until the balance tips naturally towards your spiritual work.
- Become an expert in your field, but understand that you will never know everything.
- Set yourself a definitive goal and take positive action towards achieving it: be clear about where you are heading. Keep on keeping on—you must be focused, persistent and determined.
- Give and do your best at all times.
- Find someone who believes in you and what you do.
- It is hard work to succeed—fulfilling and joyful work, but hard work. Be prepared for this.

Rachel Scoltock

Rachel runs her business Angel Psychic Healing. She's an angel psychic, energy healer, teacher and author. Born in Jersey, Rachel now lives in Australia's New South Wales in a small country town. Amongst the services offered by Angel Psychic Healing are energy healing, distance readings, workshops, events and Reiki (angelpsychichealing.com).

"My practice is called Angel Psychic Healing, and this is my 9th year running it. I fully support myself with my home-based business by offering healings, readings, guidance counselling sessions, workshops and seminars. I also do online readings and regularly travel to lead workshops. I first came to Australia in 1996 as a backpacker and fell in love with the country—I felt that I was meant to be here.

My working life began in a banking investment position after I left school as a very shy girl with no clue about what I wanted to do. My parents guided me to the 'good' bank job. I did not enjoy the work and wanted to help people, so I applied for a job at the Social Security Department where I stayed for about 5 years. It was a stressful, harsh environment; I was sick almost every day before I went in due to my anxiety at the pressured and negative environment. I did not fit in!

I left for another public service job in a venue management and marketing position. This was the first job I loved, and I stayed there for another five years until I left to backpack around the world in 1996. I enjoyed organizing music concerts, but the bureaucracy and island life was not fulfilling and I felt there was something more out there for me. After nearly three years of travel back and forth to Australia and various casual jobs to support myself, I decided to go for residency here. I knew I had to be in Australia: I felt connected, and had a deep spiritual awakening whilst here. I loved the wilderness and the indigenous culture.

I was always interested in personal development, healing, and psychic and spiritual subjects, and I have used oracle cards since I was 19 years old. But, it was never more than a pastime when I was struggling with personal issues. I was intuitive, but it was sporadic, and I was so sensitive that I found life hard at times.

Angelic guidance

My career as an Angelic Healer really found me: I had a profound angel intervention experience in 2001, followed by many other signs and synchronicities. I heard voices calling my name, found that I was becoming even more sensitive, and I saw coloured lights and heard disembodied music around me. Around that time I bought a deck of angel cards that had an advertisement saying the author was coming to Sydney for a seminar. I attended, and learnt that all the strange unexplained things that had happened to me were down to my angels. I asked for help, and then life (and my angels) took it from there.

I attended this author's next event a year later, which was a three-day workshop. I had no idea what would come of it but I just had to be there. I discovered that I could give accurate readings and messages and that I could hear the angels. On the drive home from that workshop it struck me that all I wanted to do was give readings and healings from the angels. It was like a light going on, more like a revelation and a relief; I finally knew what I was meant to do.

I realized I could not immediately support myself by doing readings. I lived in a rural area and it would take time to attract clients. I rang a local college to ask about massage courses on a whim, and their course began the next day. I hesitated as cash was tight, but they offered me a payment plan. I attended that course and a few months later I qualified as a massage therapist. I printed leaflets offering Reiki, massage and readings, and put them everywhere. I did a mailbox drop in the local area offering low price massage—and then it began.

My decision coincided with a cleansing; I immediately went off alcohol, coffee, and meat and I became a vegetarian and began to reduce my sugar and caffeine intake. This was a way of heightening my vibration for what was to come—but it was relatively easy to do. Many of the people around me did not understand, but I simply did not feel attracted to toxins—and that included some friendships, too. Nine years later I am still happily alcohol, meat-, and coffee-free, and I do not take any sort of medication or smoke.

Sadly, my husband did not support my career choice, which widened the rift that was already between us. He left around this time, which was very stressful. I had no savings or income, except my newborn small business, and I was not entitled to government help as I was not yet a resident. It was a low moment, but looking back, we had not been married long and he was obviously not right for me. I just kept going and tried to heal myself as I enjoyed my solitude and my pets.

Self-belief

In retrospect it was an initiation. I had to survive and I was so committed and dedicated to my business that I remained focused on my vision. I felt that if I got a part-time job I might split my energies too much, so I relied entirely on income from the business. I had some very poor months and became quite frightened at times. I am grateful that I had an understanding landlord as I hit rock bottom once or twice. I would not recommend that path to anyone, because you do need support.

My marketing was relentless—I leafleted and put homemade posters everywhere. I kept a mailing list and worked on myself nonstop. I learnt how to manifest and how to trust. I had to learn psychic protection: I became drained easily so needed to maintain my energy. Spiritual healing and energy healing both use a different level of energy, and it is easy to burn out. Now, I am spiritually strong. I believe in faith and trust. We are always learning and life is never a constant—just when you think you have it in the bag, something else challenges you. But I trust my intuition and psychic messages, and I trust in my angels and in God. I have faith and a healthy optimism about life. Of course I don't know it all and never will, but I know that our angels are with us all the time!"

Rachel's tips on moving into Angelic Healing

- Talk to your angels and guides every day. Ask them for guidance to give you the steps, open doors and connect you to the right people.

- Study. Gain knowledge on the subjects that interest you by reading about them and attending high-quality classes.
- Reiki is a good way to begin your journey in the spiritual sector as a healer or spiritual advisor, as it heightens your vibration and is a great basis for all healing.
- Practice! Do as many readings and healings as you can for friends and family, and ask for their feedback to increase your confidence and technique.
- Work on clearing your own emotional baggage. I had to do a lot of emotional detoxification on this journey, letting go of fears about money, about what people think and releasing negative beliefs about myself and others.
- Focus on physical self-care, and free your body from toxins such as alcohol, caffeine and cigarettes.
- Set clear intentions.
- Remember your work is about serving God, the Light and your clients.
- Practice psychic protection and remember to set clear boundaries.
- Find support: a therapist, mentor, or coach to whom you can offload and receive positive feedback. It can be a lonely road at first.
- Don't worry about competition—instead, focus on what you are doing and on doing it well. You will soon develop a good name if you are professional, caring and service oriented.
- Don't over give: many healers give too much and charge too little to start with, and then become disillusioned when they attract people only too willing to sap their energy and never pay.
- Remember you will still need to pay bills and feed yourself, just like anyone else—so set your prices to reflect your value. If you set them too low, people will think you are not worth it and not come. Be reasonable as well, and look at

what others are charging and set your prices near or in the middle.

Angelic intervention

"In 2001 I was travelling home from a festival in my car. I was alone and it was raining. I was about a quarter of the way home when I heard a strong male voice telling me to "Stop". I turned down the music and opened the window, but saw no one. So I kept going. Straight away the voice came again, louder, so I slowed down. Around the next corner I came upon an accident that had happened a few moments before: a car had gone over the mountainside; two others were stopped in the middle of the road. Had I ignored the voice, I would have surely crashed into the cars with horrible consequences. As it was, I just crept past them and went on my way, feeling a sense of shock.

A few weeks later, I awoke to hear the same male voice calling my name. This continued on and off for months and I began to find feathers on my doorstep every day, and heard strange music late at night. I later learned that these were signs that my angels were getting in touch with me. The male voice was Archangel Michael, whom I now work with every day in my healing practice.

On my way home from the first angel seminar I attended in Sydney in 2003, I hesitantly and silently asked my angels for help carrying my bags as I walked up a steep hill to a bus stop. This was my first attempt at asking them directly for anything. Within seconds a bus pulled over in traffic behind me, even though cars were parked along the pavement and the driver honked his horn. I turned and saw the driver signalling me to come over—I was shocked. He offered me a lift and took me to the station. He commented that he felt an overwhelming urge to help me, even though I had my head down and my back to him when he spotted me.

The angels get through even at the darkest moments. I was on a very awkward date once with a guy who took me to see his ex and her new man. She was not all that happy to see us, and the silences were long and painful as we four struggled to converse. I prayed for an early exit and then smiled to myself when a white fluffy feather floated over my head and landed on the barbeque plate. We left within minutes and I felt comforted that my angels were there.

A few months back I took a trip to outback Australia. My luggage failed to arrive on the baggage belt at the airport. I needed to be at my first accommodation before dark. I was starting to feel desperate when I heard the words "Go to the terminal" in my left ear. I went and a helpful young man was waiting with a message that my bag had gone on the wrong flight. He quickly organized for my luggage to come to my accommodation later on.

I hear my angels talking to me all the time, especially if I really need their help and particularly in my guidance and healing sessions. I see angels around people, and feel their presence and messages within my body and emotions. I receive channelled messages often as I write or give readings. It took me a while to completely trust and allow these messages, and to discern them from my own mind and feelings."

Mary Jac

Mary's business, Tranquil Waters, is based online. She offers a wide range of services, including personal angel readings, Angelscopes, angel cards, and inspiring quotes, advice and knowledge across her four websites, which all also feature beautiful spiritual artworks. (tranquilwaters.uk.com; myangel-cardreadings.com; pocketfulofangels.com; embracingourangels .com).

"The youngest of five children, I was always the academic one at school and excelled at maths and English. So it followed that on leaving, I went straight into a career with a well-known high street bank. Throughout most of my adult working life, I naturally progressed through jobs that were finance and administration orientated, often with a PR aspect. I used my communication and promotion skills, which I really enjoyed, but often felt that my career choices were simply things that I was accustomed to, rather than a vocation. Nevertheless, I accepted that it was 'what I did'.

I gave up work in 2002, when my husband became terminally ill. I floundered for a long time after his loss. My life changed dramatically, and so did I—and I knew that it was unlikely I would go back to a 9 to 5 job.

A sensitive soul

I've always been able to feel the presence of lost loved ones, and more so after my husband passed away. I mostly kept my beliefs and convictions to myself as they weren't shared by family or friends. But, I was swayed to explore my beliefs further after my long-passed Nana appeared to me at a time when I was at my lowest point, a few months after my bereavement. It was an amazing experience and one that I will never forget. I don't know how I would have moved on without her help.

I was also told by a trusted and reputable medium at that time that I had, "a lot of important work to do." I had no idea what he was referring to then, but knew straight away that it was a significant statement of fact—one that has stayed with me to this day. I started to work with angel cards throughout the following year, doing readings for friends, family and myself, and quickly realized how accurate my readings were. As my own Spirit healed over the following years I continued to learn more about the angelic realm. I felt that I'd formed a close bond with Archangel Chamuel and Archangel Raphael, too. I know that both of these wonderful beings have helped and supported me through good and bad times over the past few years.

Alongside my growth in spiritual awareness, I also developed a growing love for collecting spiritual artwork from the Internet, and in 2008 decided that I would like my own website to display the art collection so that others could enjoy it, too. I was given the first site as an early Christmas gift that year — and that was to sow the seeds of my new career.

Creating a business

I know that I was divinely guided with angelically channelled inspiration — ideas were coming almost faster than I could assimilate them, and as a result the site quickly grew to include my own professional personal online readings service, as well as free angel guidance cards that people could choose by instinct for those who were looking for guidance, but couldn't afford to pay for my services.

It's in my nature to want to grow and learn, and with all the ideas and information my angels were giving me, I wanted to keep expanding the website and make a second one, too, but just couldn't afford to keep paying someone to make alterations and add new pages for me. To overcome this problem I decided to learn to write websites myself, using free online schooling. It wasn't easy and I still probably don't write a site in the same way a trained expert would, but the sites work and I now have four!

The main website 'My Angel Card Readings' is now huge and I'm proud to say it averages more than 3,000 visitors every day, with people gaining their free angelic messages and guidance in several different ways as well as having access to many other pages offering inspiration.

In the summer of 2010 I was definitely helped by my angels to create my angel message cards, 'A Pocketful of Angels'. I self-published them by saving the funds I'd earned from the personal readings. The cards have proved to be very popular and are regularly sent worldwide by mail order, as well as being stocked by many shops and wholesalers across the UK. I followed these with my *Embracing our Angels* book, which is fast catching up with the cards in popularity. I love writing angel blessings and poetry, and now write annual and monthly Angelscopes too, some of which have been featured in a national spiritual magazine. I have had other magazine articles printed, too, and am constantly inspired to write more! I'm currently co-creating a range of Angel Essences with a friend as my latest project. My work is never ending but very rewarding.

Pure intentions

I truly believe that those of us who work with angels have a duty of care towards our clients and a duty of respect to the angels who make it possible for us to do so. We should never forget that they are all to be thanked for giving us the opportunity to work in such wonderful careers. I have great faith in my angelic connection, coupled with the knowledge that if I stay true to my beliefs and ethics and follow the path I am shown, my angels will continue to help me build a happy and meaningful career. I keep a positive attitude, and always believe that I'll be helped and given guidance to overcome difficulties. As a person, I feel certain character traits really help me with my work. I have a caring nature, good communication and writing skills, motivation and discipline in my working life.

Although I absolutely love what I do, being self-employed isn't always an easy route, and I would advise anyone starting up to be totally confident in their abilities both spiritually and in a business sense. Be prepared for a lot of hard work promoting both yourself and your business. Always follow your instincts and inspired ideas, but try to keep a business head on your shoulders, too."

Mary's tips on moving into Angelic Healing

- Register your business immediately with the tax office to avoid any confusion.
- Always keep your books up to date and be aware of how

much you should be putting by for tax to avoid any money concerns.

- Employ an accountant to help you with anything you are unsure of, such as tax returns.
- Get your prices correct from the start. Always be aware that they shouldn't be too high, but don't be tempted to cut your prices too much as you have to earn a living, too.
- Be disciplined when tackling the work at hand, especially if you are working from home, as it's all too easy to be tempted to put things off.
- Use a social network site such as Facebook to start a business page to support and promote your work. It's an invaluable tool that can provide you with a worldwide market, and you will make a lot of friends, too. Remember that all of the people who connect with you on Facebook are people rather than simply business opportunities. It's important to treat them as friends, and you'll find that you will gain a lot of respect from them that way.
- You don't get paid holidays or sick leave as a self-employed person, so unless you have a partner happy to supplement your income or other personal financial means, taking time off can be difficult.
- Be prepared to put a lot of hours and hard work into getting established, remembering that success rarely happens overnight.

Angelic blessings

"I am very fortunate in that I am sent signs from my angels all the time, from white feathers to butterflies, music and much more. Sometimes these come at very significant times when I am in need of reassurance or guidance; often I see them as confirmation that I am on the right path. I've been privileged to have been touched by angels, seen my own Guardian Angel and had a vision of Archangel Raphael, too. How truly blessed by angels am I?"

Donna Swan

Donna Swan is happily married and a mother to four children. Living and working in England's Kent countryside, she runs the Mardon House Healing Centre in Kent, where clients can go for Angelic Healing, healing training, yoga classes, sound healings, gong baths and Divine Healing treatments (donnaswan.com; ascendingangels.com; +0044 1732 823 811; donna@ascendin-gangels.com).

"I am an Angelic Healer, Kundalini Yoga teacher and Reiki Master, experienced in Angelic Healing and Ascension Healing and trained in remedial massage. I am also a regular facilitator of 'Empowering Events'. I have been working in the complementary health field for more than 16 years and I'm still very happy and excited to be doing so. I am a co-founder of the business Ascending Angels, which I set up with Caroline Sharp, my healing and business partner. My company has been spreading its wings all over Europe and in the USA — we've been sharing Angelic Healing attunements with clients in France, Spain, Germany, Italy, South Africa, New York, Houston, San Diego, Ontario and New Zealand, as well as at home here in London and Kent.

My work uses a combination of healing tools that support the healing of the client's mind, body, emotions, spirit and soul. The focus of my work is to make sure my clients feel happier, more physically comfortable, clearer and more relaxed after enjoying a series of Angelic Healing treatments or after attending a healing event.

My early training was as a co-facilitator of numerous women's healing workshops in both England and the USA, and I've led women's circles in London and the South East for many years. I also trained for three years in Vibrational Medicine with the highly respected Jack Temple. For more than 15 years I've been teaching all levels of Reiki, Angelic Healing and Ascension Healing to students, and supporting them in their growth and development to higher levels of connection, consciousness, self-empowerment and achieving greater joy.

A creative career

As a young woman, I was naturally drawn to acting as a profession, attending Loughborough University to study for a BA (Hons) in Drama, after which I went to drama school in London. I loved feeling free and creative, and I knew I couldn't do a 9 to 5 job or office work; I had to feel flexible in my work and life.

I reached my early 30s and realized that I was struggling and unhappy. I came to understand that I chose acting because I had a deep need to feel loved, but I also knew that when I came to have children I'd want to be at home with them to support them and be present with them as they grew up. So, acting as a career had to go. I knew I had to change directions and after much reading and contemplation I began to train in remedial massage, which then led me to Reiki and to becoming an energy healer.

Funnily enough, years earlier when I was 21 and at university, I had a friend who was a medium. She did a reading for me one day and insisted I was wasting my time going into acting, and that I was here to be a healer! It took me 12 years to get there. Being an actress involved much self-reflection, self-criticism and self-judgment. It was time to get out, to love myself instead and to do what I was good at: understanding people and helping them with their health and personal development.

When I first left acting, I trained, trained and trained. I trained in remedial massage and worked as a masseuse. Then I trained in all three levels of Reiki to Master and worked as a Reiki healer and masseuse. I also trained in other healing modalities, including vibrational dowsing and Indian head massage.

A bright light

Then, one day, the angels starting talking to me and channelling through me. I was with a dear friend when it happened, Caroline

Sharp. The two of us were giving each other some Reiki healing—and suddenly a huge light appeared in the room before us. We were blown away, we were in awe, we couldn't quite believe it but we both saw it, and then this 'light presence' spoke to us. It told us it was an angel and that it had come to teach us and to bring a form of Angelic Healing to this planet. Some of the Archangels' names we had not even heard of—we had not really been involved with angels before this. But after these meetings with the angels, we felt freer, more loved, safer and cared for—it was an extraordinary healing journey, which tremendously increased the power of the healings that I was sharing with clients and friends.

On this particular night we cried, we healed and we felt unconditional love for the first time. Then every week when we met with each other, an angel, Archangel or an Ascended Master would come to us and speak to us. They gave us healing and healing attunements to share with others. It was only after a whole year of this weekly communion and loving connection with the angels that we decided to set up Ascending Angels to share with others the words, guidance, and healing attunements of the angels. From this time forth the healing treatments for my clients became more and more powerful, and the clients were enjoying the sessions and feeling happier and happier.

Becoming a healer

It takes time to set oneself up as an Angelic Healer. It takes time to build your reputation and to attract the clients that will benefit from your work. I was married and my husband was working too, so we had two incomes and that acted as a buffer. If I had to pay the mortgage on my own it would have been very tough. But with time, practice and experience, the angelic healing work gets busier and more successful, and new ways of working become viable.

We have now put together a whole series of angelic and

ascension meditations so people don't even have to be in the same country to benefit from the healing power of the angels—they can just sign up online and listen to the meditations in their own home.

Both patience and trust have been the most important qualities for me. I had to trust again and again—trust that all would be well, that the healings would get stronger, that clients would come, that there would be enough money to pay the bills and that I was good enough. I also had to learn strong boundaries. In the early days someone would come in with a bad hip, and they would leave feeling great, but I would walk around with a sore hip for a couple of days. I had to learn to be strong, clear, honest and caring. One must not care too much; one must not try too hard. One must learn to be relaxed and trust. Everything took time. It is a journey!

Spiritually, I have surrendered myself to the angels and to the 'good' of the universe. I listen to my inner guidance and accept my intuition as a form of communication from the angels, and that I am powerfully connected to the divine flow of angelic love, wisdom and healing. I meditate regularly and I have hope. Huge hope. I believe we can all grow, love and shift to become happier, fulfilled humans experiencing love and joy here on earth. I believe in Heaven on Earth."

Donna's tips on moving into Angelic Healing

- Train well and thoroughly.
- Go gently with yourself: don't push anything or anyone.
- Listen to and trust your intuition and inner voice.
- Always listen to the angels' guidance.
- Keep healing within yourself.
- Trust.
- Set your intention and let the universe help it come to fruition.
- Be patient.

- Get some business cards made and do as much free advertising as possible.
- Know your value and therefore how much to charge.
- Don't promise anything to clients.
- Get business insurance for the Angelic Healing and any other complementary therapies you are trained in and offering.
- Create a beautiful space within which to work, including a good treatment couch and nice towels. Have lots of peaceful music to play during healing sessions.
- Make sure you conform to the rules and regulations for healing.
- Join a professional healing organization.

In conclusion

- Clear your own emotional baggage before you start to do so for others—people will sense your light and energy and will be drawn towards you if you work on yourself first.
- Don't rush—take your training and development one step at a time and trust that the angels will show you the way.
- Train at a reputable school, such as the Diana Cooper School, to gain a solid qualification and ensure you will be able to get insurance once qualified.

Chapter 5

Crystal Healing

Crystals

Practitioners work with crystals for many reasons, be it to heal, protect, energize or calm either ourselves, other people or animals; or, we may use the stones to balance, clear or attract different types of energy to rooms, businesses or homes. Minerals are able to hold, emit and amplify different types of energy, therefore working with and understanding a large spectrum of gems will allow you to unlock your greatest potential in terms of the healing and clearing work you carry out. Crystal Healers often feel a great connection with their stones, as the practice is far from one-sided since the gems actively work with the healer. Due to their myriad and individual properties, crystals sometimes feel like coworkers and helpers as well as healing tools.

When choosing a crystal to buy, it is always best to visit the shop in person rather than purchasing online as this way you can feel the energy of the stone yourself and select one that feels right to you. Always cleanse the crystal after you've bought it. Cleansing can be done by leaving the stone in the moonlight overnight, leaving it in salt water, smudging it with incense or a smudge stick such as sage or leaving it under cool, running water for half an hour. The best method for cleansing will differ with each stone, so check this before deciding on which to opt for. It's also important to regularly cleanse crystals that absorb negative energies following their use.

There are so many ways to work with crystals, from creating a crystal net or grid whereby specially selected stones are placed around the patient, to sleeping with one beneath your pillow, to making elixirs and performing rituals. You can carry them with you in your purse, wear them as jewelry, place them on chakras or meditate while holding them.

Here are some popular crystals and some of their uses; bear in mind that each stone will have many different properties that you can tap into:

- For balancing and stabilizing energy, cleansing, and purifying, fluorite is a great stone to use.
- Black tourmaline is often used to dispel negativity, while orange tourmaline is good for creativity.
- Rose quartz can help heal broken hearts, and promote self-love and a peaceful emotional state.
- The sunny stone citrine promotes optimism and cheer-fulness.
- Malachite is a protector, and is often taken on journeys or used to help keep children safe.
- Celestite is great for mental clarity and comprehension, as well as for communicating with the higher realm.

Crystal Healer case studies

Silvia Winterstein

Silvia Winterstein was born in Germany and is currently based near Perth, Australia. She opened her crystal healing and reflex-ology business—Silvia's Healing Place—in April 2011 (silvi-ashealingplace.com.au; info@silviashealingplace.com.au). Here is her story, and how she ended up embarking on a career in healing.

"I was born in Germany in 1963 and grew up near Munich. I have two sisters and even though I had a loving mother, my father was not—so, for the most part my childhood was not a happy one. I had the opportunity to leave home when I was 16 years old. From the age of 17 to 22, I lived in Munich; I then left Germany and lived in England for four years. In 1990, I emigrated to Western Australia and have lived here ever since. My first marriage, to an Englishman, broke up after six years. I then got married for the second time and had two children. This marriage was largely an unhappy union, and I left when my children were five and six years old. I have spent the past 10 years in and out of the family court, which has been difficult and disruptive. However, I had the great fortune to meet my third husband John one year after the separation. We have been together for nine years now, and he has been and still is the most wonderful man, my best friend and my great love. Most importantly, he and my children have a loving relationship.

My journey into healing started when I was a child: I had two serious illnesses that required hospital admission at the ages of eight and 13; it was those experiences that led me to my nursing career. I began working in a hospital at the age of 16, commenced my training at 17 and qualified at the age of 20 in 1983. I spent four years after that working in Munich. It was not easy to get my qualifications recognized in the UK at first. It took time. So I started working in nursing homes; I met some wonderful people there and enjoyed my work. I was a quick learner and a hard worker, and once I attained my UK registration I was soon in charge and on call regularly. I then moved to a nurse in charge position in a neurological hospital and worked there for two years. In 1990 I moved to Australia. They were great times. Plenty of staff, a lot of education, I loved it. I started in coronary care with the exception of a 10-month period working in oncology in Germany.

An alternative path

As the years passed, nursing began to feel more and more unfulfilling. I didn't like the ignorance of some medical staff in regards to complementary and preventative healing methods; I disagreed with keeping a human being alive at all costs no matter how much they suffer; I felt staff were ignoring the patients' emotional and spiritual needs—and ignoring the fact that death is a part of life. Also, at that time I was going through a difficult period in my personal life. The ongoing struggle in the family court lost me time that I could have spent with my children. I was devastated, but struggled on. I decided that now was the time to do something about changing my career and make something good out of a bad situation, and I settled on Reflexology. I discussed my plan with my husband, and as always he has been my greatest supporter. I was lucky—because he'd been in business himself for many years, he could give me a lot of practical advice on how to run a business.

So, I enrolled in a diploma course for Reflexology. With the view of eventually starting my own business around that time, I also became interested in crystals—I was first drawn to their beauty. I discovered that science would not be where it is today without the use of crystals, and I started to learn about their healing powers. I enjoyed learning something new immensely, but I still hadn't dealt with all my negative baggage, such as the years of acrimony with my ex-husband and the family court.

Healing myself

It was a devastating time for me despite my husband's love and support, and I became very depressed. It was necessary for me to take antidepressants for a while, as well as therapy. There was a short time when I just wanted to give up, but I decided to be kind to myself and allow myself time off to heal, no matter how long it took. This was one of the best things I ever did. It was OK to feel sad for a while; deep down I had the belief that it would pass, just like the flu. I continued to read about the healing powers of crystals and began meditating—which was new to me—using crystals during meditation. Then, I woke up one morning and knew it was time to stop taking the antidepressants. I continued my work with crystals and was certain that my emotional, mental and spiritual health would return. And so it did. To me it was quite miraculous; it seemed I had to experience the healing power of crystals myself before I really believed. With a newfound vigour I completed my Reflexology diploma. I also wanted to learn more about Crystal Healing with the view to eventually incorporating it into my business. I thought it was important to do some formal study, so I have since completed a Crystal Healing and Advanced Crystal Healing course and a pendulum-dowsing course.

I believe that if one is passionate about something, one will always succeed. My strength is that when I feel weak or sad, I think about those times I overcame obstacles in my life I never thought I would. I draw on my experiences where I showed great strength and courage, overcoming my fears to accomplish something, or to be kind to others or to myself. Spiritually, I have always believed in a higher being that is pure goodness; I like to call it the Divine. I believe that evil only exists because people decide to be that way. It is a choice and not some unknown force. I believe that kindness and love attract the same."

Silvia's tips on moving into Crystal Healing

- Educate yourself, and read a lot.
- Practice, play and work with crystals.
- Share your experiences.
- One crystal healer wrote in her book what prevents a lot of people from becoming great healers is that they don't follow their intuition. This stuck in my mind, as it is so true.
- You can't do anything wrong as long as your intentions are good.
- Share your passion but don't try to convince non-believers. Passion is contagious and people will come to you—you will be surprised.
- Be patient.
- Starting a business is not easy, so keep at it.

- Get practical free advice from your bank and from business associations.
- Set a treatment room up at home if you can; if you don't have the space, start off by being mobile and doing home visits.
- Advertise in holistic or health journals.
- Set up a website; it's great exposure.
- It takes time to get known and build up clients. For me the best way was to continue to work part-time; that way I didn't have to worry about making money.
- Believe in yourself and look after yourself.

Heather Prince

Healer Heather Prince also teaches relaxation and meditation. She has always felt a connection to Spirit, and thanks to a series of events, was drawn into healing, which has changed her life. Heather feels a strong connection to the angelic realms and feels the energy from Archangel Michael with his sword of courage, and Archangel Raphael, the healing Archangel, around her. Her son, an Indigo child, led her to write a self-help book on the topic (heatherprince.co.uk; heather@heatherprince.co.uk).

"My life has been steered by an unknown force. As a child, my introduction to the spiritual world was through my parents—they were interested in spiritualism and attended spiritual church meetings, even though as a family, we are Jewish. For me, those meetings proved without a doubt that there is an afterlife. Aside from this, I experienced more personal things: I 'knew' without knowing how, about people who were dying and about pregnancies and what sex the baby would be. I was very sensitive to atmospheres. It was natural for people to seek me out and ask advice on their problems. I had a school friend whose father was a well-known medium. When I spent Christmas with them at the age of 15, I felt someone stroking my hair and surprisingly, it didn't freak me out! In fact, it was somewhat comforting.

I met my husband, who I now understand is my twin flame, at the early age of 15; our relationship has been my biggest learning curve. We separated after 28 years of marriage and are now getting divorced. But he has been one of my main teachers in life; he taught me to stand up for myself, love myself and to know that I deserve respect. I bless my time with him and our three wonderful children and our granddaughter.

My working background is in journalism—I worked for a time at IPC Media on *Titbits* magazine. My passion was definitely writing, and I created short stories for the weeklies, but never got them published. Eventually, I left *Titbits* and went to work for the Director of Editorial Development. When I was pregnant with my first child, I accepted voluntary redundancy and left to be a fulltime mum.

Turning point

In my early 30s, with three young children, my old school friend's husband was diagnosed with cancer. At this difficult time, I thought hard about whether there was something I could do. I thought to myself, there must be. In the end, I went to visit Rita, the lady who served in the local chemist—my parents knew that she was a healer. She invited me to sit in her development circle, although I wasn't certain at the time exactly what that was! I watched and learned as she performed absent healing. Initially, I was so spooked out—I cuddled up to my husband in bed that night and watched every shadow! I didn't return for months, but Spirit had other plans for me.

One morning, I woke up with a wry neck, which meant I couldn't turn. I rang Rita and she saw me immediately. After a soothing healing session I could move. Amazing. She asked me to return and when I did, there was a client with chronic arthritis. Rita asked me to give healing. "What, me?" I asked laughing. "Not me." "Yes," she insisted. I put my hands over the lady's knees and could feel heat coming from my hands and after a little while they became cold again. It was if someone had flipped a switch. I continued training every week for the following two years before becoming a full member of the Jewish Association of Spiritual Healers (JASH).

Becoming a healer

During this time, I was certainly tested. For seven weeks I suffered with a blown disc and was completely bedridden. But, faith in my belief of healing with a little help from an osteopath got me well again. So, what did I learn? Compassion for others who are in pain. And, that time in bed gave me the opportunity to study many books. I went on training courses with Forever Living Products and learnt about nutritional supplements and how diet affects your overall health. There are so many facets to the overall holistic aspects of healing, but I couldn't earn a living through it, so I returned to work as a bookkeeper and studied at the same time.

My gift turned out to be leading the visualization meditations during the psychic development circle time, so I began my own small group from home. It grew quickly and my husband suggested I should hire a hall. The space hosted by my Slimming World group looked suitable; I asked if I could hire the hall and have been using it for my work ever since. Some people thought the hall had an unpleasant vibe, but after my groups began, people would mention that the vibe had changed and it felt so much "lighter".

A new outlook

Healing has changed my life. My research into why my youngest son behaved in certain ways led me to understand about Indigo children, and to a woman who trained me as a Spiritual Response Therapist. This awesome therapy works by removing blocks and negative energies from the Akashic records. I mentioned to her that it would be great if there was a book I could give to my son to explain about who he was and the role he had chosen in his life. I wanted the Indigo kids to know how special they are, but not in respect of being 'abnormal'. So, she suggested I write one! And therefore, *I am Indigo* was written—a self-help book aimed at Indigo kids.

My passion is to help people reach their full potential, and by running meditation classes twice a week, organizing an annual retreat, running workshops and reaching more people with my CDs and books *I am Indigo* and *The Rainbow Within*, I am able to do this."

Heather's tips on moving into Crystal Healing

- Train with a reputable healer and join a reputable organization so that you can get insurance.
- Always remember that you are a facilitator and that the energy you use comes from Source.
- Meditate, focusing on knowing that the work will flow and asking for guidance.
- Work on yourself with love and forgiveness first and foremost before working with others.
- Learn counselling skills—even though your business focuses on crystal or energy healing, quite often people will also want a friendly ear to talk to.

Helen Meyrick

Helen is a holistic therapist whose specialisms include Crystal Therapy, Reiki, meditation and Reflexology. Her business, Dreamstone Therapies, is still expanding and currently offers courses and workshops in Crystal Therapy, meditation, Reiki and IT for therapists— her original career path was in IT and software programming (dreamstonetherapies.co.uk).

"When I was at school, everyone seemed to know what they wanted to do—go into teaching, nursing, become a doctor, but I didn't have a clue! I heard someone talking about the Computing Science course they were doing, and decided it sounded interesting. That's how I began my career in computing. I worked on and off in this industry for 27 years. For 11 years of that period I was a full-time mother, and during that time I felt I really lost my identity. I was searching for something to explain who I was and what I was doing here, and that is when I first became interested in crystals and complementary therapies. I visited my local Mind, Body, Spirit fairs and made regular appointments with a Reflexologist and my interest was piqued.

In 1999 I began working as an IT Consultant. The job involved working away from home, staying in hotels or company-rented apartments, long hours, lots of driving and heaps of stress. It was then I really started to develop my interest in holistic therapies. Any opportunity I had, I visited shops and fairs where I could buy crystals; the contents of my bookshelf began to change from fiction and 'techie' books to titles such as *The Crystal Bible*, *Every Woman a Witch* and so forth. I began to feel empowered and also found an escape from the stressful world of database management. The first workshop I attended on crystals was with Denise Whichello Brown and it was a crystal massage workshop—I was hooked. I signed up to do Anatomy and Physiology, followed by VTCT Crystal Therapy. I wanted more! Alongside this I had also discovered Reiki and signed up to do Reiki Level One with Lorraine Rees from Reiki Wales (reiki-wales.co.uk) without even ever having received a Reiki treatment myself. I felt like I had been invited to a banquet, and there was so much on offer. I was hungry for as much as I could have. My crystal collection continued to grow as did the number of books on my shelf, and in addition I was growing spiritually and in confidence. In 2005 I felt that the ethics deployed by the IT company I worked for no longer felt right and I gathered up the courage to hand in my notice and trust that the universe would point me in the right direction.

Great enthusiasm

I contacted Lauren D'Silva at Touchstones Therapies (touch-stones-therapies.co.uk) about the Institute of Crystal and Gem Therapists (ICGT) crystal therapy courses she ran, and signed up as I felt that I wanted to do more work with crystals. In addition, I did my Reiki Master Level—although I was in no way ready to teach anyone.

A few times I tried to 'start up' a business and paid to rent slots at a therapy room. On one occasion I got badly burnt in the business sense by a woman that I had trusted. I eagerly (and naively) parted from money that I could ill afford by advertising scams, believing I was signing up to have my business advertised on appointment cards in a local surgery.

So I decided to take things more slowly; I figured the universe was giving me that advice too, as for a number of years whenever I had aura or card readings I kept getting told I should be teaching. I kept resisting until I was offered a part-time job teaching IT in adult education with the proviso I did a Postgraduate Certificate in Education (PGCE) course, which, as it turned out, has been of a great benefit as I moved more into teaching Reiki and crystal work. The teaching qualification has given me the confidence and grounding in how to format workshops and courses and develop resources. And that is where I am today.

After a lot of nudging and shoving from the universe, I am on my path—and every day I am still learning something new, gaining knowledge and developing spiritually. Yes, it has been bumpy at times and sometimes it seems like I'm going nowhere or I'm going backwards, but I am getting there, gaining recognition, creating an ever-growing circle of like-minded friends and acquaintances and noticing the synchronicities and opportunities being presented to me—and that is the key for me: follow the signs!"

Helen's tips on moving into Crystal Healing

- Don't expect instant success—it takes time to start up any business, and you should make allowances to pay out more than you make for quite a while. If it's meant to be, it will happen: just persevere.
- The best sort of advertising is word of mouth and being visible. Skip taking out expensive adverts in magazines or newspapers and instead get out there at MBS fairs and events.
- Keep a stock of business cards and leaflets handy to give out at every opportunity—these are easy and cheap enough to get made up online.
- Make use of free advertising on the web though directory listings and social media sites.
- When it comes to training, ensure that the courses you study are reputable, accredited, insurable and provide plenty of practical experience. I initially wasted money on online courses—but nothing is better than attending a class, getting practical experience, creating a network of fellow students and enjoying the support of a good teacher.
- Invest in membership of a recognized professional body such as the Federation of Holistic Therapists (FHT) which will provide you with credibility and support.
- Believe! In yourself, and in the fact that if you are on the right path—the opportunities will present themselves (although maybe not in the ways you expect).

Ashley Leavy

Ashley is based in Madison, Wisconsin, in the USA and offers online classes as well as workshops through her business the Love & Light School. Courses include a range of energy healing modalities such as Crystal Therapy, Reiki and Aromatherapy. She also offers distance healing (crystalhealer1.webs.com;

crystalhealer1@gmail.com).

"I have loved crystals my whole life. When I was younger, my grandfather would take me to gem shows and teach me about all the different minerals. I was always captivated by their beauty and I soon began to collect and learn about stones. My grandfather had a big influence on me and to this day I share his love of nature—rocks, plants and animals. I had a great interest in plants and horticulture and earned my Associate's Degree in Ornamental Horticulture. When I decided to pursue a Bachelor's Degree, I was feeling a lot of societal and family pressure to choose a major (and occupation) that would be respected and profitable. As a result, I chose to go into Botany. I forced myself through a year of unfulfilling coursework before I realized that the only occupations I might realistically find in the field were with pharmaceutical companies or creating genetically modified organisms (neither of which felt right with my innermost beliefs). I knew it was time for a change.

A new opportunity

While I was in college, I was lucky enough to find a part-time job at my local New Age shop, Mimosa Books & Gifts. I found myself drawn to study a variety of spiritual and natural health topics (all the while neglecting my university course work). It was then that my passion for crystals was renewed. I began taking some certification classes in Crystal Healing (the first of which was with one of my mentors, Akeeya; it was Melody's Laying-on-of-Stones Levels One and Two). That changed everything! I knew in my heart that this was the change that I was looking for—this was the path that I needed to take. I had finally found something that I truly loved. It was a way to combine my interests and beliefs with my profession. When I was growing up, I was told that I could be anything—a firefighter, a ballerina, an astronaut, even the president of the United States—but no one ever told me I could be a Crystal Healer. I spent the summer break working at Mimosa and giving Crystal Healing sessions to clients. Then, my dream really came true; an ownership position opened up in the shop and I was approached by my now current business partner, Diane, about becoming a co-owner. We went through a trial partnership period (which went great) and I made the decision to buy into the shop. Needless to say, I didn't return to school the next fall—I was already living the dream! The shop and my Crystal Healing practice went hand-in-hand and things were 'in the flow'.

After doing sessions for a few years, and after years of self-study and lots of professional training in Crystal Therapy, my clients began requesting that I teach classes on Crystal Therapy. So, I began giving free Crystal Healing lectures to local spiritual groups and women's circles, working my way up to short, donation-based events. I finally had enough teaching experience that I was approached to teach a 13-part crystal series by a local healing arts school. I now travel over a wide area offering a diverse range of classes and I have also created an online, virtual classroom where I teach students from around the globe. This has really tied in with my New Age shop and each of my businesses feeds and supports the other—for example, my customers at the shop often enroll in classes and my online students often order supplies from the shop. My hope is that they will continue to grow and evolve in harmony.

Striking a balance

At first, it seemed difficult to juggle the demands of the shop with my healing and teaching practice, but with experience, I have found the right fit. I have also had to remember to take time for myself and for my family—starting (and operating) any business can be a bit demanding of your time and energy, so staying focused on the present moment, and what is truly most important in that moment, is key. The thing that was most difficult for me to overcome was the social pressures I was facing to pursue a more traditional career. It was challenging to find my own voice and work through this challenge, especially when I was feeling unsupported by friends and family. I didn't want to disappoint anyone, but I knew that if I didn't at least try to follow my dreams, I would always regret it. So I went for it, worked hard and here I am now, living the dream!

I would say that my strengths are compassion, the ability to be direct and that I am purpose-driven. I am dedicated to what I do and I am able to trust in the energy that I am working with. I feel connected to crystals and to the natural world in a deep, spiritual way.

Ashley's tips on moving into Crystal Healing

- Believe in yourself and in your healing gifts.
- Know that the rough spots don't last forever.
- Learn as much as you can—continuing education offers new techniques to better serve yourself and your clients.
- Staying centered and grounded can help bring you clarity when you need it most.
- Be authentic—your clients will appreciate it and will like you for you.
- Don't underestimate the power of client referrals; offer your existing clients a special bonus or discount if they refer you to a friend.
- Be prepared to work hard—starting a new business, or developing an existing one, takes time and commitment.
- Partner up with colleagues and other people in your industry—share, support one another and co-create together.
- Don't get discouraged (for long) and NEVER give up—you CAN do it!

In conclusion

- Keep learning as much as you can, as possessing extra

skills related to Crystal Healing will help you to provide your clients with a better service—as well as expanding your knowledge base. A course in counseling would be a good choice.

- Offer existing clients a discount if they introduce a friend to your work—the best sort of advertising is word of mouth.
- Keep practicing with crystals whenever you can find the time.

Chapter 6

Psychics and Mediums

From those who practice their art for free with family and friends to people who have made a successful career out of their gift, Psychics and Mediums hail from all walks of life and operate in many different settings, from their front room to halls full of hundreds of people. Many have been born with their ability or have a family history of psychic sensitivity, while others have developed it as their lives progressed.

Psychics use clairvoyance to peer into the future, and may use instruments such as Tarot cards or a crystal ball to aid their work. They could also possess mediumistic skills allowing them to contact those who have passed over. Psychics are often blessed with telepathic skills, using an extrasensory ability to pick up on feelings, perhaps knowing when a friend is in trouble or that a family member is about to call. Clients may ask for guidance on their relationship or career, perhaps they want to make contact with a deceased loved one or simply come for a reading for the fun of it!

Mediums are also psychic, but they can also see into the past as well as the present and future, and can make contact with those who have passed over, as well as Spirit guides and angels. They deliver messages from the dead to the living—this area of their work is extremely popular. Some specialize in certain fields, from Spirit clearing and guiding lost souls to the light, to helping detectives solve a murder case that's seemingly reached a dead end. They may work in a spiritual church passing messages from the other side to audience members, or conduct private readings in their or their client's home.

Psychics and Mediums case studies

Ian Lawman

Exorcist, Psychic and Medium Ian Lawman is best known for his appearances on *Most Haunted* and *Living with the Dead*. His psychic abilities came naturally to him, and after a career as a model, dancer and fighter he moved into the psychic world after an appearance on the *Psychic Live* show in the early 1990s. He now runs ghost hunts around the country in well-known haunted hot spots such as Pendle Hill (ian-lawman.com; +0044 1162 538 668).

"Regarding my psychic career, things just fell into place for me. I finished school with no qualifications as I was a bit of a bad boy! Then, after I'd finished my career as a dancer the only thing I could do at the time to pay my mortgage was to read the Tarot. A journalist contacted me as he'd heard I'd left my career to start a new path in the psychic realm — I was one of those interviewed, and from that point on things started to open up slowly for me. The journalist was from Scunthorpe, UK and was fascinated that I had gone from being a fighter to a dancer to a spiritual person.

The 'David Beckham of Spirituality'

I started going to a spiritualist church, because although I understood Tarot and clairsentience, I didn't yet know how to harness and direct my deeper understanding of spiritualism. Moire Moore, the president of my spiritualist church in Ashby, started my spiritual career — she called me the 'David Beckham of spirituality'! I attended her spiritualist circle and within 10 minutes I was receiving information. That gave me confidence, because before, when I was reading the Tarot I was always questioning whether I was truly seeing things or whether I was being a psychologist, fitting my readings to my client. I also began to see the difference between my own voice, and my Spirit Guide's voice — at this time I was roughly 24 years old.

Surprising reactions

The main setback I experienced in this industry is jealousy—I didn't realize how gossipy or unspiritual it could be, even within the spiritual churches. Even when you sit in a circle for the first time, some people might tell you it takes one, three or more years to progress—yet within six weeks of starting I was working in a rostrum in different spiritual churches.

The other challenge was image—as a Psychic Medium people have an image of what you might look like. With a skinhead and tattoos I didn't fit that idea and people judged me before they'd spoken to me. The church wanted me done up in a suit and tie, which apart from weddings and funerals, wasn't me, so I stood my ground! This was something Moire, the president of the spiritualist church in Ashby who helped me on my career path, told me. She explained how people would give me advice, but I should only take what I want on board because sometimes people give the wrong advice due to jealousy. I listened to her, and I always hear her words today—she died in 2013, aged 90.

Fighting spirit

My personal strengths come from being an ex-fighter: I don't suffer fools gladly and I'm outspoken, but not in a negative way. I know when people are feeding me bull—and I let them know that I know. I am honest with everyone, and I expect people to be honest with me. It doesn't take much to be polite, or kind. Also, I'm able to tell when someone means me no good: I'm able to 'read the punch' that's coming! I believe you get out of life what you put in—put 100% in and you'll receive the same back.

Act with kindness

Once, I was travelling to a ghost hunt and in the same train were about 25 to 30 soldiers. On got an old soldier with a host of medals on his chest—he was struggling to carry his luggage, but not one of these guys offered to help him, so I ran over and assisted him with his bags. A little later, a girl recognized me and asked for my autograph. The veteran noticed this and asked me, he hoped I didn't mind, but who was I? Was I an old soldier? I explained what I did. He said to me that he couldn't believe that someone who wasn't ex-military had gone out of his way to help him yet the others didn't—he bemoaned the young generation, which I thought was so sad. I believe you should treat people how you would want to be treated.

Always be honest and truthful with people. Help them— simply start with helping those around you with their day-to-day life in whatever way is useful. Be kind to people. Spirituality is a calling—you can't just 'go into it'. Once you're kind and nice to others, the path will open up to you; stay away from those who are negative. The web is full of these people, those who believe they are spiritual but are actually negative, and they fail fast.

Importantly, understand that everyone needs to start off small; I'm 44 now and have been doing this since I was 25. A lot of people see the success that I've had, or Derek Acorah, Colin Fry or Tony Stockwell, and expect the fame and money to come straight away. Be patient.

Angelic disbelief

When I was 'Buried Alive' at Dudley Castle, something happened that made me question my cynicism about angels. I believed in angels, but at the same time I wondered if some people imagined them being at their sides during hard times. Talking to a live radio feed on day four, I was suffering both emotionally and physically. Jacky Newcomb called in and said that the angels were watching over me. After, I thought that the last thing I needed was some 'airy-fairy' person! Then, a white feather landed on my glass coffin lid. I told Jacky. I checked with the security guard as there was a zoo nearby but the curator of the castle and the zoo said that the feather did not belong to any bird that they knew of nearby, and it wasn't a seagull's as they wouldn't fly overhead due to the hawks that were flown at the castle. It was the width of my thumbnail and about 2 inches in length with soft downy feathers, and I still have it."

Ian's tips on moving into the psychic business

- Take a look online, ask around and research respected people within your line of work—talk to as many people as possible in your field.
- Research the local area and the people you're going to be up against.
- Think of ways you can differentiate yourself from others.
- Before you quit your employment, start part-time, as you may need time to get established before you can go full-time.
- Be prepared to work for free at the start.
- Be prepared to travel many miles.
- Remember—you don't have to be famous to be at the top of your field.

Nina Ashby

Nina, a Psychic and Medium, works at Psychic Sisters in London's Selfridges. She gives psychic readings, aura readings, clairvoyance, mediumship, card readings, past life overviews, insight and strategies, and is a career and relationship specialist. She runs readings face-to-face, over the telephone or on Skype and also offers parties, group work and development courses (ninaashby.com; nina@ninaashby.com; +0044 20 8410 4846).

"I have been working as a professional Psychic since 1980 using many types of spiritual disciplines. I was born in New York and educated in the US. I am an extremely lively, eternally curious and outgoing person. I believe in learning and asking lots of questions in life (not in readings!) and empowering others. I have always been 'Avant-Garde' and have had to endure a lot of puzzled criticism from others who just have not been able to understand why I had to do things that did not make conventional sense to them, but perfect sense to me.

Clear vision

From an early age I knew I saw the world differently from those around me (literally!) and that it was not really acceptable to speak about it. Being very artistic gave me an acceptable route to express myself and I decided to become an artist at the age of eight years old. To be an artist is to keep your vision open and, through your work, to open others' vision and sense of a different way of being. Actually this is a perfect description of what I still do as a reader and healer, though using a different set of vehicles.

My move to a career in the spiritual and healing sector was very organic; it was certainly never something I considered as a young person. I am a multi-talented person and it was art or languages that intrigued me intellectually. I have never worked in a 9 to 5 job, and as a self-employed person I have always had more than one income stream running at the same time.

Multi-skilled

Prior to becoming a full-time professional reader I was a Vibrational Healer, Licensed Massage Therapist and teacher of massage and energy healing—and prior to that a professional Sculptor and a Medical Secretary. Every profession I have engaged in I have been passionate about and, in retrospect, I can see a progression and interface between them all.

I eventually became interested in esoteric matters and alternative methods of healing in my late teens, and began serious study in my early 20s, developing a voracious appetite to learn and practice at the same time as pursuing my art career. Meditation, astrology, palmistry, energy healing, herbalism, nutrition and diet, esoteric color and yoga were some of my passions. Since the age of 15 I have taught what I know: art, French, massage, energy healing and esoteric and spiritual development. It is a passion and a natural ability that I have been privileged to use.

At about the age of 28 I decided I wanted to stop working for doctors as this did not excite me anymore, but I had doubts about really being able to earn a viable living as an artist. I thought hard about what I loved to do and so decided to train to become a masseuse. That was pretty unusual in the 1970s! From that moment on I became almost instantly successful as a massage therapist and body worker, because I was able to incorporate the personal knowledge and skills I had been developing in the esoteric field throughout the previous years.

Laying the foundations

My clients called me 'golden hands'. The more body work I did the more my aura vision became usable to me, and I began the process of putting together my knowledge—I had so many amazing experiences and insights working energetically that I began to share them with my clients. This gave me the means to test my perceptions and to get feedback. They then started to ask me to give them readings. I began studying with a spiritualist medium in Montreal who opened up my channeling abilities as well as giving me the opportunity to start giving readings formally, and to teach classes in auras and energy and psychic development. This formed the foundation for the training courses I still teach to this day.

A new start

I was told by my Spirit Guides to go to London, where I subsequently met my husband. I moved to the UK in 1983 and had to start all over again. This was much harder than I expected, as I had found it so easy to make contacts and friends in New York, Montreal, France and Spain when I worked or lived there. To overcome this I slowly worked on expanding my social and professional networks so that I was able to create new opportunities personally and professionally. For example, I joined the British Astrological & Psychic Society (BAPS) in 1984 and became a Consultant member. I also volunteered on their executive committee and began to network, meet and work with other professionals within the psychic field. I studied Aromatherapy and was able to meet other massage and energy therapists via this route. When I lacked friends, I joined a choir and met lovely people.

Every year I learn new things and incorporate them into my work, and there is a new balance of using my skills. Sometimes it's more involved with healing, sometimes more Psychic work, sometimes more writing and media work. I do not like a boring life and if I get restless I keep finding a new way to get involved in something that I am passionate about.

Channeling and mediumship

I use my psychic senses to perceive the discarnate intelligences around people: passed over folk, personal Spirit Guides, Spirit animals and angelic beings. They communicate to me through images, feelings and thoughts I hear in my own mind.

Passed over souls always tell me how their life ended and some memories about themselves, their life and their relationship to the person having the reading. They rarely give future predictions. I remember one lady's fiancé who was killed in a car accident came through and told her what happened to him. He had died quickly, and was confused initially. He passed on very detailed information to her and she was satisfied and comforted by his visit.

Spirit Guides have come to me in so many varied forms: pixies, elemental creatures and people from former times that have spiritual growth information and lessons to impart as well as advice. Their energy always has an uplifting effect on the vibration within the room.

Angelic Beings are huge and bright and always such a surprise when they appear to aid and comfort the individual. They often come unexpectedly and give you a short clear message and a truckload of high-level energy. I remember being at a friend's house and feeling very strange and suddenly a huge golden light came in front of me and told me to call home. I did and my husband had been taken very ill."

Nina's tips on moving into the psychic business

- Be educated—natural talent is not enough! Know your stuff and how to explain it to others. You have to be confident that you are an expert.
- See yourself as a business professional.
- Charge for what you do. Giving and receiving is a law of the universe. If you do not value yourself, others will not value what you offer.
- Be honest. Know what you can do and promise no more than that. If, within the first 5 minutes of a reading, no connection is made, admit it and stop.
- Network—join an organization, work with others, be proud of who you are and what you do and let others know what you do. Every area of your life, from meeting people in the supermarket to standing in queues can give you great opportunities to get clients. Everybody wants to know what others 'do for a living' so use it!
- Be responsible. Be aware of legislation, what you can and cannot tell people and know that clients really listen to what you tell them so be careful.
- You can't do it all! Have a list of other professionals to refer on to.
- Love what you do, love the people you work with and work in their best interest. You are the source of your clients, YOU attract them. They will reflect what you have

to offer, so be mindful.

- Keep learning. Stay interested. Be passionate.
- Keep good financial records. If you are a professional you have to declare income and pay taxes. Paying more taxes is one indicator of your success.
- Start small and grow your business. Use your frustrations to help you search for new answers and solutions to problems.
- Manage your expectations.
- Walk your talk! If you claim to be into spiritual growth, then you need to manifest it!
- There is no competition—you are unique and will attract the clients that need you. Be kind to others who work in your profession. What goes around, comes around.
- Self-employment is often cyclical and cash flow can be a problem. Make sure you have several income streams to help keep your finances healthy: readings, healing, phone lines, fairs and exhibitions, writing, lectures and small local teaching groups, for example.
- Stay aware of current trends in the business—you will mostly be working alone, so networking with other Psychics and knowing what is going on in the broader context of the psychic world is important.

Anne Marie Kell

Anne is a Psychic Medium and Tarot reader based in Lincolnshire, UK, although she also offers home visits. She uses her guides, Tarot, angel cards and a pendulum to provide caring and uplifting readings. Anne offers readings via email, telephone, and MSN and Yahoo chat (annemariekell.com; annemarie@annemariekell.com).

"Besides running my own business as a Psychic and Medium, I have four children and three stepchildren, and am engaged to a wonderful man called Paul who has been a huge support along my spiritual path. Career wise, the main jobs I have done are hairdressing and aerobics instructor, neither of which fulfilled me, yet both prepared me for my spiritual path in their own ways without my realizing it at the time.

I always had a sense of there being much more to my career path. At the age of 15, my nan, who was also a Medium, told me I would be taking her place and working like her later on in the future, to which I laughed as the whole thing scared the life out of me. I tried so many different jobs, but nothing was giving me that total satisfaction that I craved for, that feeling of having a soul purpose, and finding the job I love the most. When my ex-husband left me at the age of 30, I wanted to change my whole life. I have always been aware of Spirit but was held back from doing it for many years, and from this life-changing experience I started to learn more and develop myself.

Changing directions

My first step into the psychic sector was joining a website that offered readings from photos. I very quickly realized that I had something unusual—and I was good at it! After I met my now fiancé Paul, he encouraged me to go onto eBay and start off small, offering readings. At the time there were not many others doing this kind of thing, so it was pretty easy, and everything fell into place. I was getting great feedback, and totally loved working from there.

Competition time

The setbacks in experience were that people cottoned on to what I was offering on eBay, and slowly but surely many other Psychics came along and the whole atmosphere changed to the point of other Psychics making comments because I liked my listings to look nice. I overcame this by putting my faith in Spirit. I worked via eBay for three years, but Paul urged me to create a website and work from there and come off eBay altogether. This was a huge leap of faith; I didn't know if I would sell another reading, and I started off by advertising in other places such as free ads, other spiritual sites and link building.

Staying strong

I am not a quitter; I knew this was going to be a hard path, and I knew I would have to endure some hard times. There have been times, especially in the early days, where we lost a lot of money through advertising, but I still felt that there was so much more on this path for me. I believe these experiences have made me stronger and wiser, and more able to help other people.

I have had to overcome my fears, especially when it comes to clairvoyant nights—these I have found the hardest, being terrified of being wrong or not getting any Spirit come through. And working for two national magazines, *Soul & Spirit* and *Silent Voices*, has brought me challenges with how I write.

My spiritual strengths are that I have total trust and belief that Spirit will always look after me—the more readings you do, the stronger your psychic abilities become and this has been true for me, making my clairsentience and clairvoyance my strongest spiritual strengths.

Anne's Guide

I met my guide Godfrey in the strangest of ways; I had just come off a radio show where I had been giving free readings, and straight afterwards I needed to send a same-day reading. All of a sudden I saw this old man in a tweed jacket, who just stood beside me. I asked his name and he told me it was Godfrey; he was very posh sounding. I asked who he wanted to pass a message on to, and he just kept saying, "I am here for you, my dear." I even posted a Facebook status saying I had this strange man with me by the name of Godfrey—I didn't know anyone by this name. I started to ignore him as I needed to get my reading sent—this lady had asked if she should have an operation, and if she did would she be OK. She didn't say what it was, so I sat there tuning in to Spirit. Next thing Godfrey taps me on my shoulder! I was at this point thinking, what on earth is happening? He coughed, and said this lady is having a hysterectomy, tell her to let them whip it out, it will take years off her. I sat there rather nervously, typing out what he had said; I apologized profusely, and said if this was wrong, I would refund her and I would look at it again. To my complete shock, she came back to me, laughing her head off, amazed. She said it *was* for that operation, and she loved his expression. I sat there with my mouth open, and the rest is history. Godfrey is my guide, he helps me with my readings, and he even has his own personal slot on my Facebook page and passes messages on about the daily cards."

Anne's tips on moving into the psychic business

- If you are after making quick money then forget it—this is a lifetime commitment, and it takes a lot of hard work to get out there and become known in the spiritual sector.
- Do not waste money on advertising—in the 12 years I have been doing this, I have easily lost £3,000 with wild promises of getting clients, to not even get one call. Facebook is my most successful outlet for getting known: a great strategy is to ask followers a question to get their psychic abilities working—then whoever guesses right, treat them to a mini reading—but post it on your wall so that other people can see how good you are. This gets you a lot of attention, and will bring you a lot of sales in.
- Start off by charging a small amount, as with life as it is at the moment, not a lot of people have spare money, so do special offers. People respond more to the phrase "in-depth reading"—they want value for money.
- Learn to say no—all your friends, family and everyone you come into contact with will want a free reading. At first you

will be keen, but remember that this is your business and you need to earn money.

- Ask your clients to leave feedback on Facebook or your website—this is so important, as it is what potential clients will look at first.
- Join social sites, adding 'Psychic' or 'Medium' as your surname, so people can find you easily.
- Set up competitions for free mini readings.
- Be patient. I started in 2000 and it took six years to get to a place where I could live off my earnings.
- Post a disclaimer or code of ethics on your website—you're more than welcome to copy and paste mine, and change the name.
- Create your own working space solely for your readings.
- Take up a counselling course.
- Get public insurance.

In conclusion

- Try to offer lots of different types of services, such as readings over the phone and face to face, attend fairs and exhibitions, write articles and give talks.
- Research your local area and think of ways you can differentiate yourself from the competition.
- Create a Facebook page to engage with your followers and show how accurate you are—and ask your clients to leave feedback on Facebook or your website.

Chapter 7

Aromatherapy

Aromatherapy is the use of essential oils extracted from plants for the purposes of healing through the medium of massage. As a holistic treatment, it targets mind, body and soul and the therapist will often focus on the body's Meridian channels and pressure points. The art of Aromatherapy has a very long history, although the actual term was coined in the early 20th century. Its uses have ranged widely — from the Egyptians, who used the oils for cosmetic applications (and embalming the dead) — to Frenchman René-Maurice Gattefossé who, in the early 20th century, burned his arm and plunged it into the nearest liquid he could find, which happened to be lavender oil. His arm healed quickly with no scar, leading him to investigate how essential oils could be used for medicinal purposes — and to him coining the term *aromatherapie*.

Many believe that the treatment can aid symptoms of anxiety and promote relaxation, as well as help manage pain and treat skin complaints. The therapist will tailor the oils to their client, taking into consideration their lifestyle and physical and mental health to help improve vitality, promote a healthier appearance, ease muscle tension, boost mood and eliminate toxins.

Popular oils

Amyris: this oil has a woody aroma, with a slightly sweet vanilla tone, and is often used for stress, insomnia and relaxation.

Bergamot: this citrus-scented, fruity oil is made from the rind of the bergamot. Its uplifting and confidence-building properties make it excellent for those suffering from depression and anxiety.

Cedarwood: thought to be one of the first oils extracted and dating back to ancient times, the woody scented cedarwood is useful for building inner and spiritual strength.

Eucalyptus: this oil has an easily recognizable scent. It's purifying and invigorating and often used topically as an antiseptic, or to cool the effects of a fever.

Myrrh: known also as an ancient perfume and incense, myrrh can aid visualization and meditation.

Rose: uplifting, romantic and sensuous, this oil is intense and warm and associated with matters of the heart.

Ylang ylang: with a floral aroma, ylang ylang is a calming oil that has sensual and romantic effects.

Aromatherapy case studies

Dewi Hopley

As well as Aromatherapy, Dewi also offers hot lava shell massage, Tsuboki Japanese face therapy, traditional Balinese massage therapy, neuroskeletal realignment therapy and remedial massage and Indian head therapy. Prior to treatment, she offers a full consultation covering lifestyle and medical history. She's currently taking a break from therapy work to teach English abroad for a year to gain new experiences and perspectives, and enrich her life further.

"I set up my therapy business three years ago, starting as a mobile practitioner. Now I bring clients into my home using my therapy room. I travel abroad twice a year to attend a well-being retreat in Southeast Asia where I'm one of the facilitators—I teach massage and basic Aromatherapy. While I'm there, I also travel around different hotel resorts in the area as a guest therapist.

In earlier years, I did a lot of temping administration work to fund my travels abroad, secretarial school and university. I then decided to train as a TEFL teacher (Teaching English as a Foreign Language) as it allowed me to travel. I spent four years abroad in Indonesia (I'm half Indonesian so I guess I wanted to connect more with my roots), had a great life, great income and enjoyed it—but something was still missing.

A sweet smell

When I turned 30, something changed—I questioned what I was doing with my life; I felt I was drifting and life didn't hold much meaning. I always wanted to help people and I was tired of working hard for others and not feeling valued. Being in Indonesia helped me remember how affected I am by aromas— it's a very fragrant and pungent country! I remembered the spices my mum used in her cooking, how'd they smell and the traditional herbal oils she used whenever we were ill. I stumbled across Aromatherapy on the Internet and that's where my journey started.

I moved back to the UK to start a diploma in Aromatherapy, which took three years to complete as I had to go back to temping work to support myself financially. In that time I did other massage courses, became a lot more aware of the spiritual side of things and became more open in myself.

Making the switch

After two years temping I felt increasingly restless and really wanted to start my own business. It just so happened that the company was undergoing redundancies at the time, and that was my cue to do so. I took a leap of faith and set up my own business. It was at the beginning of the recession but I didn't care because I knew this is what I was meant to be doing. Things fell into place, yet at the same time it was difficult as I pretty much had to start from scratch again. I also worried a lot about when the next booking would be! But I just couldn't bear the thought of going back to temping or working for anyone else other than myself. It would have been easier to have had a part-time job while I started out, but it wasn't an option for me. I needed to go through the difficulty to learn what I know now. Very simply, I let go of worrying about money and just got on with doing my work. Once I let go of worry, things have flowed more.

First steps

My main drawback was my lack of business knowledge—I was never really taught how to set up a business. In our Aromatherapy course we had to research how we would go about it, but this wasn't very useful. It would have been great to have had different therapists who had their own businesses come in and talk about their experiences. If I'd had the money to go on a business course for therapists then I would have! In the end I attended a few Business Link (gov.uk) sessions, which really helped to demystify the practicalities of self-employment. I'm still learning; I've learned more through trial and error! Now, I let my business grow organically. I don't push it, or myself to excel or develop in anyway—this takes the pressure off. I follow anything that grabs my interest and see how it can fit into my business.

Spiritual tips

I meditate often which helps keep me balanced and happy—I can't stress enough how this has changed my life! Because of this, I'm more in tune with people's needs. But equally important, I honor my needs more—I come first."

Dewi's tips on moving into the Aromatherapy sector

- Affiliate yourself with people who have moved into this sector and ask them about their experiences.

- Be discerning and follow your instincts on what feels comfortable for you.
- For those in the UK, access Business Link for free advice and seminars on how to start up your own business. HM Revenue & Customs also have free seminars regarding self-employment—they're also really helpful if you have any questions.
- Get out there and do mini (and fun!) talks to local groups, for example at the Women's Institute, about what you do. Take your oils in and ask them what each one reminds them of. Make it an experience for them, as they will remember this much more than you standing there and just talking about it.
- For more variety and all round business and personal development, check out resorts and retreats that have a guest therapist program—not just in the UK but also abroad. It's a great way of gaining experience, honing your skills and meeting all kinds of people with different conditions.

Paula Dear

Paula is an experienced holistic Aromatherapist registered with the International Federation of Professional Aromatherapists. She trained at the prestigious Tisserand Institute in London after she won a scholarship in a national competition. Other services Paula offers include deep tissue massage, Indian head massage, baby massage, and speech and language therapy (pauladear.com; +0044 29 2063 0560).

"I had been a speech and language therapist for 20 years. I was working with children with multiple disabilities and teenagers with physical disabilities. I was finding the work demanding and stressful, although also fulfilling. I began to ask myself if I wanted to do this for the rest of my working life—and suddenly that seemed like a very long time!

Once I had started to question what I wanted to do next, things began to fall into place. I had been to Aromatherapy evening classes when I moved to Cardiff as a way of meeting people, and I loved it. I secretly nurtured a pipe dream of becoming an Aromatherapist—but thought people would laugh as I already had a career. A colleague at work knew how much I loved the oils and massage, and brought me an application form for a competition in a health magazine. I had to write an essay on why I'd like to be an Aromatherapist; I was called for an interview at the Tisserand Institute and won a scholarship to train as a Holistic Aromatherapist. It took two years of part-time study with me travelling down to London once or twice a month for very intensive weekends, then following it up with study and practice during the week. This was while I was still working four days a week as a speech and language therapist and looking after my family!

The next step

I was ecstatic to pass all my exams and decided that I would take the plunge and start my own business, while still working a day and a half a week in speech and language therapy. I have been fortunate not to encounter many setbacks—I planned for nearly the whole two years I trained, so I had some idea of what I was aiming for before I started. I was, however, ill for a few weeks two years ago and tried (very stupidly) to carry on. I discovered what an awful patient I am and I finally had to admit defeat, and learned from that to look after myself and not to stress about not earning money when I am ill. When I started, there was inevitably a period of time when I did not have many clients. I learned to be patient, but several things I tried, such as offering treatment packages to retirement homes, were just not going to work, and it was important to admit that and move on. After all, although I love what I do there are the practicalities of actually making a living.

Personal beliefs

I'm not someone who believes you 'get what you deserve' or 'if you want things enough they happen'—otherwise there'd be no people starving in Africa. There are so many who desperately want a better life. We are where we are and should do the best we can in the circumstances we find ourselves. I do believe in trying to see the good in all—if something isn't working, try something else. I believe in trying not to be judgmental and to do things out of love and not anger. It's great to look on the bright side, but I'm realistic enough to know that sometimes there isn't one, and you should acknowledge and not deny your feelings.

I think we should all seek a balance between body, mind, spirit and environment as if one of those is neglected then you are likely to feel out of sorts. I see Aromatherapy as addressing all four of those areas, because as practitioners we talk about clients' environments, work their bodies through massage and oils and engage their minds and spirits through the oils and through listening."

Paula's tips on moving into the Aromatherapy sector

- Fall in love with the oils—keep appreciating them each time you smell them. Know your oils, their properties and their characters. One of my brilliant tutors used to tell us to think of oils as people and assign them characteristics—e.g. ylang ylang for me is a blousy woman with a feather boa, while vetiver is an old man who smoked cigars!
- Get the best training you can afford.
- Acknowledge that you cannot be all things to all people.
- Give talks, tasters and be enthusiastic about the oils.
- Learn to massage really well. As the main route of delivery of the oils is through massage, we need to be good at it!
- Find out what your unique selling point (USP) is. Have you worked with stressed people in your previous career? Encourage them to come to you for treatment because you

understand exactly what they're going through.

- Look after yourself. Have treatments. How can you recommend things to your clients if you are not following them yourself? I have had a treatment once a month for many years; I could not cope without them. It saddens me when I go on courses and hear therapists say they have no time for treatments themselves. It's vital to your health and also you learn a lot from other therapists. Remember to use your oils on yourself—even if you cannot get a massage, try the other routes of delivery—compresses, inhalations, baths—then you can recommend them to your clients!

- Listen to that part of you that may be called God, angels, Spirit or soul—it doesn't matter what you call it, but it's that part inside of you that is sometimes at peace and happy, or sometimes shrieking out that what you're doing isn't right—don't ignore it.

- Say 'thank you' lots! To the universe, God and nature; your friends, family and clients.

- Learn, educate yourself—keep your skills fresh and up to date but don't do too many different courses until you have worked out those that increase the value of your treatments.

- Look after your hands—do a hands-free massage course to help with this—TEACH therapy run excellent ones in South Wales, UK.

- Join groups that have nothing to do with your work so that you meet more people and get to know them—word of mouth is the best form of marketing but you need big circles of contacts. Don't just join them because you think you might find clients though; do something you love—I do Appalachian tap dancing and belong to a book club.

Business tips

- Plan, plan, plan! Have a proper business plan—a course

will help you with this, otherwise business advice is often available from councils.

- Go on a free tax advice course with the tax office.
- Have a budget for marketing, equipment and courses.
- Try to accumulate some savings if you are supporting yourself, as this will give you breathing space to find clients.
- Join a professional body such as the International Federation of Professional Aromatherapists (IFPA).
- Get insurance.
- If something isn't working, change it.
- Dream, enjoy and have fun! That's why you're changing your career.

In conclusion

- Take your oils on the road and give talks before engaging with the audience, giving tasters.
- See if there are resorts or retreats that have a guest therapist program.
- Hone your massage skills by taking a course.
- Have treatments yourself—not only to take care of your health but also to learn from other therapists.

Chapter 8

Hypnotherapy

There are so many strings to the bow of hypnotherapy—happily, most people now realize that there is so much more to this fascinating profession than those stage hypnotists that can apparently make members of the audience act like chickens. Whichever specialism you choose, you will be helping people in a deep and profound way. Those interested in the more spiritual side of things may be drawn to past life regression, future life progression or between life regression—all of which often reveal fascinating accounts, and can help remove emotional blocks for your clients.

Alternatively, you may wish to help people rid themselves of additions, remove a phobia, help them to lose weight, improve their confidence or public speaking skills or deal with any other issue they present to you. Suggestive hypnotherapy helps clients to stop a destructive behavior such as smoking or become more confident doing something such as public speaking. Analytical hypnotherapy seeks to find and target the root of the problem— unlike suggestive hypnotherapy, which deals with the symptoms.

The process of hypnosis sends the client into an extremely deep sense of relaxation via which the hypnotist is able to access the subconscious in the non-analytical right side of the brain. In this state, although very relaxed, the client is completely aware of what they are saying (although their speech may slow a little), and they are able to stop the session whenever they wish. Far from feeling far away and sleepy, the client is acutely focused on the therapist's voice. The hypnotist will use their own method of taking the client into this state, perhaps asking them to count down from a high number before taking them on a visualization where they descend steps into a specific location. Then, the hypnotist will begin their session using a series of questions and suggestions.

Hypnotherapy case studies

Lorraine Flaherty

Lorraine works as a Transformational Therapist, using the tools of Hypnotherapy, NLP, past life therapy, future life progression, life between lives, inner child work and energy clearance—and also offers retreats. She's helped thousands of people—including the author—from all walks of life to overcome their fears and reach their full potential. She's a full member of the British Society of Clinical Hypnosis and the General Hypnotherapy Register, a Master Practitioner of NLP and a member of the Past Life Therapists Association. She's based in London (innerjourneys.co.uk; info@innerjourneys.co.uk; +0044 7702 253 660).

"My spiritual journey began more than 30 years ago, but around 11 years ago I got involved with Neuro-Linguistic Programming (NLP) and then hypnosis and then past life therapy. I spent years searching for something that would really make a difference to the world and the people around me, and eventually I found it. These days I get to take people on journeys into their subconscious world, to the place where all of their memories are stored—memories that can be good or bad. I then help them to deal with them accordingly—they can explore memories and experiences from the past, the future and the space between lives to learn more about themselves. The result is that they can take more control of their current lives and live more fully in the present, no longer distracted by unnecessary clutter in the back of their minds. My aim is to help people live in a happier and more fulfilling way. Whichever of the tools that I use, I feel very honoured and blessed that, every working day, I get to share incredible experiences with my clients. Their stories never cease to amaze and inspire me, and offer all kinds of invaluable insights into who we really are and why we live our lives in the way that we do.

Beautiful beginnings

Ever since I was a young child I had questions about why we were here and what life really meant. It was hard to find answers from the people around me, and, as I have always loved reading, I constantly had my head in books—about religion and secret societies, shamanism, the power of the mind and all things esoteric.

As I grew older I became a little distracted from my spiritual path and after I left school I dived into the world of hairdressing and make-up; it was a world where I was able to use my creative skills to help people look better, and, as a result, feel better. What I discovered was that I could make them look better on the outside with my technical skills, which was great and very rewarding; but the real revelation for me was that by listening to people, and by being genuinely interested in them and their lives, they felt better on the inside, too. I liked this a lot.

I became an Art Director for a chain of salons and was very involved in training and delivering seminars and hair shows. I also worked quite extensively with L'Oréal, helping them to create new products and promote them. I enjoyed this role but always felt that there was something else I was supposed to be doing; something that would be more fulfilling and satisfying, and something that could help people more profoundly than just changing the way they looked.

Turning point

A near-death experience on an airplane made me wake up and realize that I needed to make some dramatic changes in all areas of my life. After the experience I set out to explore all the things that I had ever wanted to do. I took some time out and created a bucket list, and then came back and began to implement all of the things on the list. One of them was acting, and after a stint at drama classes and some acting work I eventually decided it wasn't for me and left it to explore the world of therapy, as the drama work had shown me how lives could be improved by a process of self-exploration.

I underwent Psychosynthesis—a kind of spiritual psychotherapy—and I learnt a huge amount about myself, who I was and who I really wanted to be. I gained the confidence that I needed to step out of my old, familiar and relatively comfortable life that I had created; the one where I was always left feeling as though there had to be more to life.

I attended many classes and workshops in the UK and all over the world, learning all kinds of new skills including Reiki and some shamanistic practices. I was really lucky and got to work with some of the best teachers in the world and to have some remarkable experiences, the 'wow' moments that I think should be a part of everyone's life.

True purpose

I knew that I wanted to inspire people, to motivate them into changing their lives and reclaiming their personal power. I loved the interaction with people that the acting classes had provided me with, and I think this is where the seeds were sown of me wanting to teach. I also had a huge desire to learn how to explore other lives—past lives in particular. This had always been something I wanted to do, and the first time I explored it I had an amazing experience that led me to want to know more, and to train so that I could do it myself.

Moving into hypnosis

I decided to explore different therapy courses, but found it difficult to decide on the right place to go. I learnt Reiki and I loved it—but it didn't feel as though it was the right thing for me.

I am, and always have been, a believer in getting signs from the universe. So when everything I read and almost everyone I spoke to, over a six-week period, mentioned NLP—I decided to learn more about it. I hadn't realized that this was to be my route into hypnosis.

The first time I put someone into hypnosis, on my NLP practitioner course, it felt as though it was something I had done all my life—it came so easily to me and the results were astounding. I was invited back as an assistant on the NLP training courses and spent many years helping Paul McKenna and Richard Bandler, the co-creator of NLP, teach it to others. I recognized that I needed to know as much about it as I could; and when I eventually found the right school and the right teachers, I studied Clinical Hypnosis for about four years.

Inspiring others

Once I was qualified and had developed a successful practice I was invited to teach hypnosis to medical students, midwives and dentists all over the country—and at universities, including Oxford and Cambridge. I particularly loved having the opportunity to demystify hypnosis and prove to those in the medical world that hypnosis really does have its place. The response from the students was amazing. I was able to alleviate their stress, which helped them revise better and as a result do considerably better in their exams than they had done previously. I became quite popular with the students, if not the faculties of the colleges, who were concerned that my teachings might have been a little 'kooky'.

It is wonderful to know that future generations of doctors will be aware of the power of the mind, and the connection between the mind and the body.

Doing what I love

Once I began to explore past lives with my clients the results were astounding, and it led me to explore future life work and the life between lives, which just got even more incredible and interesting.

I found that the more I allowed myself to do the work that I adored, the easier it was for it to happen; doors just seemed to open and the phone kept ringing. Even though I am not, and never have been, the best at marketing myself, I have always been busy—and as I continue to learn more and more and advance my skills the clients that I see just keep becoming more and more amazing, and the changes that happen in their life happen quicker and quicker.

So little time

At the moment, I don't have enough time to do all the amazing things that are available to me; I have so many ideas and feel as though I need to be split into many parts to get it all done. I love to see my clients, write books, produce CDs, run workshops— and on top of that there are so many people to learn from and experiences to have myself. There never seems to be enough time to get it all done!

To overcome this I have put some aspects of my personal life on the backburner, but this is something that I have done consciously, as I feel that right now it is more important for me to be of service as best I can, at a time when the world is in a transition state. Once things settle down during the next few years, I will think of ways to make more time for the other areas of my life.

Lorraine's strengths

I think that my biggest asset is my passion and belief in the work that I do. I am completely determined to learn everything that I can about people, and will keep learning more and more ways to help them be the best they can.

My biggest spiritual strength is 'knowing' what I believe in is right. I have always known, without any shadow of doubt, that people have everything that they need right inside them; that there is a spark of light—a divine spark—that connects all beings and the earth. I believe that we are all incredibly powerful and that all we have to do is to remember who we really are and recognize that strength and power within so that we can be whoever we want to be."

Lorraine's tips on moving into Hypnotherapy

- In order to succeed you have to believe in yourself.
- Create a great website.
- Writing a book generates credibility.
- Doing talks generates respect and interest in you and your work.
- Be prepared to put in time and effort—this may require letting go of some old ways of being and even, sometimes, people that have been in your life.
- You need to have a sense of determination to succeed, no matter what, and the energy to make things happen.
- Have a plan.
- Be prepared to fail sometimes and to learn from mistakes and move on.
- Learn to trust your gut instinct, as it is always right.
- Become good friends with your bank manager and be organized.
- Keep your promises and don't offer more than you can deliver.
- You need to be able to ask for help, sometimes, from those with skills that you do not have.
- Be honest and always work with the best interest of your clients at heart.
- Read lots!
- Discover how the most successful people got to be where they are and follow a similar path.

- Investigate training centres; find the ones with the most credible reputations, and the ones that provide the best qualifications at the end of the training. Speak with the teachers and see if you feel comfortable with them.
- Practice, practice, practice on anyone that you can to build the best skills.
- Do not give up your day job straight away—begin the process slowly, working part-time, and then allow your business to build.
- Keep learning and improving all the time.
- Research and keep up to date with new developments.
- Take time to clear your own issues so that you can be the best therapist you can.
- Meditate and take care of yourself mentally and physically.
- Connect with peers for support and new learning.
- Find a good mentor.
- Surround yourself with positive, inspiring people.
- Stop watching the news and reading papers; become more selective about what you absorb.
- Focus on gratitude for all that you have in your life.
- Always strive to be the best that you can be whatever you are doing.

Karen Richardson

Karen is a qualified counselor and Hypnotherapist accredited by the British Association of Counselling and Psychotherapy (BACP), the British Institute of Hypnotherapy (BIH) and the British Strategic Therapy Foundation (BSTF). She has three facets to her work: one-to-one and couples counseling working across London using techniques including Clinical Hypnotherapy and Cognitive Behavioural Therapy (CBT) to help alleviate a range of issues; she works two-and-a-half days of the week counseling students with an 'open-door' policy at the school; and running her company RCAssociates (RCAssociates.org.uk) whereby she gives presentations to students and parents at schools on a variety of relevant subjects such as bullying (karen@karen-richardson.org; +0044 20 7431 0456).

"I grew up in Middlesex, UK, and was the third of four children—three girls and a boy, born 18 months apart. At the age of eight my family life changed dramatically when my older sister was badly burned. From that point on my parents' attention revolved around my sister and her recovery. My brother, sister and I were left to our own devices. My parents had fixed ideas about the type of job my siblings and I should have. It was expected that my brother would go into the family business, construction, which he did—and that my sisters and I would become secretaries, get married and have babies—which they also did.

My career, however, did not follow the course my parents had planned. In my early teens I decided to become a model and at 17 I left school and went to the London College of Fashion where I attended a one-year modelling course. On completion, I pursued a career in modelling until I got married at the age of 22. I was quite successful in my career, but it never produced feelings of fulfilment. At the age of 23, my first daughter was born and I moved with my husband to Antigua in the Caribbean and started a business finding locations for modelling and film shoots on the island. It was a fun job that fitted in well with bringing up small children.

Life change

By my mid-thirties and three children later, two girls and a boy, I was divorced and moved back to the UK. I realized that with bills to pay it was time to go back to college and retrain for a career that I would find fulfilling—something in the caring profession, such as osteopathy. After a one-year Science Foundation Course, I enrolled in a four-year osteopathy course at the British School of Osteopathy. Two years into studying I became ill and had to leave. At the time I remember feeling like a failure. A year later, I enrolled for a three-year Person Centered Counselling BA course at the Metanoia Institute, and also for a Hypnotherapy course at the London College of Clinical Hypnotherapy (LCCH).

Moving into hypnotherapy

My decision to study hypnotherapy was influenced by a consultation I had with the late Allen Carr in the early 80s in order to give up smoking. During the consultation I was convinced that I was not being hypnotized. In fact, I left there thinking what a waste of time that was, but 11 hours later I was surprised to note that I hadn't even thought of smoking a cigarette.

Before I found the right course to study I researched the various options available and looked for one that was accredited, near to my home, affordable and with a timetable that would fit in with bringing up three children. Having found the LCCH course I had no difficulties enrolling as I already had the required qualifications from the Science Foundation Course I had taken. During my training in hypnotherapy I also had a counselling placement at the Equilibrium Centre for Counselling, which allowed me to offer hypnotherapy to my clients, thereby providing me with lots of practice and giving me the opportunity to hone my hypnotherapy skills.

The only real difficulty I faced was that the hypnotherapy course was at weekends, taking me away from having quality time with my children and requiring me to find someone to look after them, which I did.

Faith and dedication

I would describe my strengths as stemming from my enjoyment of working hard. I am persistent, focused and determined as well as result orientated; however, not to the extent of being driven to attain those results at all costs. My spiritual and personal lives are intermingled; I have a loving spirit that is warm, affectionate, open and accepting of others. I have both belief and faith, and I express awe, wonder and reverence throughout the day and at weekend trips into the countryside. I always try to be my very best, which includes practising forgiveness, empathy, congruence and unconditional positive regard."

Karen's tips on moving into Hypnotherapy

- Research the business geographical area well.
- Get to know every aspect of the competition: their qualifications, their offerings, their pricing structure, their 'special offers', their facilities and their means of promotion and marketing.
- Invest in a website, leaflet, advertising and web-based professional directories.
- Find practice rooms which charge by the hour, or a fixed fee by the client—and where other non-competing therapists work from so that there can be cross-referral.
- Have a professional phone answering service; clients tend to book the first therapist that answers or returns their phone call.
- Visit local GP surgeries to offer counselling services and encourage referrals.
- Be 'client-centered'—there is nothing worse than listening to a therapist blow their own trumpet. It's all about the client—not you.
- Add more strings to your bow—find other opportunities where your skills may be of need and exploit the commercial opportunity. This is not only financially rewarding, but adds variety, interest and fulfilment to your life.

In conclusion

- Keep up to date with new research and developments.

- Connect with peers for support and the opportunity to learn from each other.
- Find a therapy room where other non-competing therapists work from so that there can be cross-referral.
- Ask your local GP for referrals.

Chapter 9

Top tips

As you make the transition into your new, dream career, here's some all-round advice that may help you out:

Look after number one

Care for yourself physically and emotionally first and foremost. You cannot offer healing to others if you are not at your full emotional and physical potential. Life will always throw you curve balls and you will most likely need to deal with personal problems as you enjoy your holistic career. It will be important for you to be able to react and deal with such challenges, and being physically and emotionally fit will help you with this—as will your guides and angels. If you wish, cut out potentially harmful substances from your diet, such as alcohol and sugar, and try to give up cigarettes if you smoke. Take regular exercise to keep your body strong and your mind sharp and clear. If you feel as if you might need someone qualified to help you talk through emotional issues, consider looking into counseling or speak to your GP for advice.

Another point to remember is that people are coming to you in most cases for healing or help. Some of these people will be in delicate emotional or physical states, and they're putting their trust in you to treat and heal them. You may find yourself acting the counselor or guide—sometimes your treatments may inadvertently incorporate talking therapy! Perhaps you could use your life experience to help clients, or undertake a counseling course.

Community spirit

Join groups in your community that are unrelated to your chosen field of work—this way you can chat about what you do and make friends, which may help with potential feelings of isolation once you start to make the transition into your new career.

If you want to run courses or give healings, remember that face-to-face isn't the only way you can do so. Aside from the telephone, you could also use Skype, which allows you to video chat with clients for free, or offer online courses.

Know your worth

Before you get going, practice your art on as many people as you can—friends, family and colleagues will probably be thrilled to help out. Once you've got your business started, always charge what you're worth—it may be tempting to give away freebies to friends but, particularly as you start up, you need to remember that you also need to make a living as well as healing and helping others. However, if someone is on a low income, is a student or a pensioner, you may wish to offer a discount.

Keeping up appearances

Make your therapy room or business premises as aesthetically pleasing and welcoming as possible. Decorate it in calming colors, use incense or burn essential oils, offer complimentary natural teas, fresh water and juice, create a relaxing waiting area with magazines and comfy chairs, and if you're using a treatment table, invest in the comfiest one you can afford.

Communicate

If you can find the time, use your expertise to teach others. Hold workshops to pass on your skills, or do talks at your local community center to share your experiences, answer any questions people may have about what you do and help to inspire others.

Similarly, writing articles, blogging or even writing a book will give you even more exposure and help to strengthen your credibility even further. If you want to pitch an article to a magazine, always find out the name of the person you're pitching to—often the commissioning editor or deputy editor, as the editor will probably be snowed under—and keep your pitch to a few concise lines as well as including a short bio of your achievements and qualifications. Give your contact a call in a week's time if you've heard nothing back, as they may have missed your email. Even if the answer is no, you have still made contact and, if your idea isn't right, the editor may be impressed by your knowledge and be interested in future ideas. The key is to keep in regular contact with the magazine, so that your name sticks—this way, they may think of you first if they need an article written on your subject.

Chapter 10

Alternative alternatives

Here are some other therapies you may be drawn to—and expert advice from those in the field on what you need to do to get started.

Reading the Akashic Records

The Akashic Records are stored in our universal consciousness—they are an energetic imprint of everything that each soul has ever thought, said and done, and also hold future possibilities for that soul. Each person has their own individual entry, and anyone can train to access the records. Therapists may access their client's record to help them learn about their soul path, or heal emotional issues.

Expert advice from AJ McClary, Professional Intuitive from ajmcclary.com

Do I need a qualification?

The Akashic Records are an energetic database that certain Psychics are trained to access. Doing so positions your consciousness at a vibration where you can connect to the client on soul level, so you usually focus on clearing blocks and restrictions from present and past life trauma currently affecting the client. It is difficult to learn the proper techniques from a book alone, so training is usually passed down as a lineage from teacher to student.

How can I find a training course?

I studied with Slade Roberson (sladeroberson.com), Susann Taylor Shier (soulmastery.net) and Anne Brewer (anne brewer.com) to name a few. Many of us study with multiple teachers. Other teachers include Andrea Hess of Soul Realignment (soulrealignment.com) and Linda Howe of Akashic Studies (akashicstudies.com). I completed my training online, with telephone support.

What do I need to set up a practice and roughly what will my costs be?

Training starts around US$600, but an advanced practitioner can expect to pay up to $5,000. Other expenses include setting up a website, blog and newsletter.

What is the best way to attract clients?

One of the best strategies a new practitioner can use to attract clients is by offering a teleseminar once a month—I make this offer to the participants at every event.

(ajmcclary.com)

Aura reading

As living beings, we each have an energy field that surrounds us. Aura readers are able to see this field and the colors it is made up of. Each color represents a certain emotional or physical aspect of our personality, and the reader will be able to translate what they see to their client, and explain what the colors mean for their emotional, physical, spiritual and practical life.

Expert advice from intuitive aura reader Jennifer Lynne Flint, at The Painted Universe

Do I need a qualification?

I'm sure it would be possible to find someone who provides some form of certification, or offers courses on seeing auras. But I don't think most people expect a formal qualification. Where intuitive readings are concerned, reputation and experience are probably more important. Clients just want to know that you can do what you offer, and that you can help them with their personal transformations.

How can I find a training course?

There are books on the subject of aura reading, and I've even found apps that claim to train you to see them visually. I am an intuitive aura reader, though, so I perceive auras in my mind rather than externally. I think it's perfectly fine to train yourself! I use things like Hemi-Sync binaural beat music (check out hemi-sync.com), meditation and psychic development games such as guessing playing cards to help strengthen and maintain my abilities. It's also useful to practice reading friends, or you can ask someone to send you photos of historical figures you don't know, and see what you can discern from their auras. This is a terrific way to develop your skills for free. I sometimes post this kind of exercise on my blog at jenniferflint.com, as does Anna Sayce at psychicbutsane.com. It's a lot of fun!

What do I need to set up a practice and roughly what will my costs be?

That depends on what kind of readings you want to do. If you're meeting clients in person, you may have expenses in maintaining a space to do so. But I conduct mine via photo and email, and there is virtually no overhead to that at all, aside from promotional materials such as business cards. All you really need to get started is an Internet connection, a PayPal account and the ability to do the work. Pretty simple!

What is the best way to attract clients?

I started out by offering readings by donation through my blog, and established a reputation that way before setting up a more formal practice. It's helpful to maintain a list of current and former clients, and interact with them by email, blog and

Facebook so that they remember and recommend you. Ask for testimonials after each reading as well. From a metaphysical point of view, I think it's important to know what kind of clients you typically attract, and why. I suspect that on some level everyone is an aura reader, and that's how my clients know I'm the right reader for them. It's a matter of instinct, and it's okay to let that work for you. Imagine the perfect clients, and the universe will manifest them for you!

(jenniferflint.com; info@jenniferflint.com)

Herbalism

This is the study and use of plants for therapeutic purposes, to help strengthen and heal the body. It is an ancient form of therapy and many of today's allopathic medicines are actually based on ingredients derived from herbs.

Expert advice from Dalbir at Pure Herbal Healing

Do I need a qualification?

Herbal Medicine today requires you to undertake an accredited degree in Herbal Medicine. Students will usually also undertake a minimum of 500 hours of supervised clinical training. Medical Herbalists are fully trained in Western orthodox medical diagnosis and treat their patients holistically as individuals.

How can I find a training course?

These can be found through The National Institute of Medical Herbalists (NIMH) (nimh.org.uk), the American Herbalists Guild (americanherbalistsguild.com), the European Herbal & Traditional Medicine Practitioners Association (ehtpa.eu) and the National Herbalists Association of Australia (nhaa.org.au).

What do I need to set up a practice and roughly what will my costs be?

Setting up a practice can be done from home or as part of a complementary clinic. You will need an initial outlay of your herbal dispensary, which includes your herbs in various forms, i.e. tinctures, dry herbs, creams and salves, as well as stationery for patient records and the usual office equipment required to run a business.

What is the best way to attract clients?

Social media, local newspapers, flyers, talks and your own website.

(Pure Herbal Healing, 21 Kelmscott Road, Birmingham, B17 8QW, UK; pureherbalhealing.co.uk)

Reflexology

Reflexology is a type of massage that is applied on the feet, lower leg, hands, ears and face, focusing on certain pressure points on each of these areas. The treatment is tailored to the client and the aim is to restore balance to the body and mind, leading to a greater sense of well-being.

Expert advice from Sally at Footworks

Do I need a qualification?

Definitely yes. You cannot be recognized by any professional or statutory body or be eligible for insurance cover without a recognized qualification. I would always recommend training through the International Institute of Reflexology (IIR) if you're in the UK (reflexology-uk.net) as this trains you in the Original Ingham Method, which to me is the best. The IIR qualification is recognized worldwide. You must belong to a professional body such as the Association of Reflexologists (AoR) (aor.co.uk), the British Reflexology Association (BRA) (britreflex.co.uk), the Reflexology

Association of America (reflexology-usa.org), the American Reflexology Certification Board (arcb.net) or the Reflexology Association of Australia (reflexology.org.au).

How can I find a training course?

For those in the UK, contact the AoR and they will give you a list of all the recognized training courses. Alternatively, browse the IIR website for details of their training courses. In Australia, you can find courses at the Australian School of Reflexology (reflexologyaustralia.com) and in the US, the Reflexology Association of America (reflexology-usa.org).

What do I need to set up a practice and roughly what will my costs be?

There are three basic routes to setting up depending on your circumstances. Firstly, you can work from home, which has a huge cost benefit as you won't have to pay rent. But, you need a private room and your house is on display to all your clients, so it always has to be tidy and the bathroom immaculate. You could also run into issues if you have children or pets. The second option is to offer mobile visits. You'll need a reliable car and one that is big enough to accommodate all the gear you need to take. The time it takes between home visits is lost time, and every house you go to is different and can be tricky. The benefit is you don't have to use your own home! Another important issue is personal safety when visiting new clients. Always say where you are going to someone at home. The third option is working within a clinic or multidisciplinary practice—this is great for referrals from other therapists, your room will be ready to use and there may be a receptionist to organize bookings. The downside is that it can be very expensive—most clinics charge for room time whether you use it or not.

You'll need to budget for insurance, a website, equipment, stationery and marketing.

What is the best way to attract clients?

Website, website, website! Other methods are doing a leaflet drop, getting involved with fundraising events at local schools, and advertising in your local church magazine—this is cheap and effective and has brought me loads of local business. Also, tell everyone you meet you are a Reflexologist, be prepared for them to ask you what it is you do and always have business cards to hand.

(sallysfootworks.co.uk; info@sallysfootworks.co.uk; +0044 7796 908890).

Shamanism and shamanic healing

Shamanism might be considered the world's oldest spiritual practice. Over tens of thousands of years our ancient ancestors used shamanic methods to contact sources of wisdom and power, not just to benefit themselves, but to bring healing, knowledge and practical wisdom to their peoples. The word 'shaman' (pronounced SHAH-mahn) comes from the Tungusic-speaking peoples of Siberia and north China. It generally indicates a person who is able, in an altered state—most often achieved through rhythmic percussion sound or sonic driving—to leave his or her body and travel to other realms to interact with spirits.

Shamanism is a holistic healing method and shamans in both indigenous and contemporary settings address the spiritual side of illness and injury in a complementary relationship with non-spiritual treatments. Shamanic healing is a spiritual healing practice, and training alone does not make one a shaman.

Expert advice from Susan, President of the Foundation for Shamanic Studies

Do I need a qualification?

You do not need a degree or other credential. However, good shamanic healers are typically mature with substantial life experience, conscientious, compassionate, ethical and grounded. They are interested in helping people, as well as animals and the natural world. Most have successful careers in other disciplines, including the medical profession, business, alternative healing and psychology. Typically, because it is an intense spiritual healing practice, practitioners have other professions in addition to their shamanic practice.

How can I find a training course?

Founded in 1979 by Michael Harner as the Center for Shamanic Studies, the Foundation for Shamanic Studies (FSS) offers training programs in shamanism and shamanic healing across America and worldwide in Canada, Europe (shamanic studies.net), Australia, Latin America, and Asia (shamanism-asia.com/shamanism; including Taiwan, Japan, Indonesia, and Thailand). A complete description and schedules of FSS training programs can be found at (shamanism.org). For those in the UK, visit The Sacred Trust (sacredtrust.org; offers Foundation for Shamanic Studies trainings) or Second Sight Healing (second-sighthealing.co.uk); for Australia there's the Australian Institute for Shamanic Practitioners (shamanicpractice.com.au) — and worldwide training can be searched for at Shamanic Teachers.com (shamanicteachers.com).

What do I need to set up a practice and roughly what will my costs be?

Get the best training you can and practice what you have learned. When you feel ready, set up a private space to offer shamanic healing one-on-one to clients. All that is required is a private, quiet, simple space with room enough for two people. Some practitioners do this from their homes, some have a small office space. The major costs for practitioners are for high-quality training. Shamanic practitioners typically have one or more drums and rattles, and whatever other tools they have gathered throughout their training and practice.

What is the best way to attract clients?

Get the best training you can and achieve success with your
clients; word of mouth will then bring you all the clients you
need. There are also many websites where you can list your
services—including (shamanism.org). Shamanic healing services
can be marketed just as one would market other alternative
healing practices, although a clear description of what shamanic
healing is needs to be provided.

Thermo-Auricular Therapy (Hopi Ear Candling)

This technique works by lighting a hollow candle and placing the
unlit end at the ear canal; this forms a suction to remove
impurities from the canal.

Expert advice from Pam Bennett

Do I need a qualification?

Before taking a course you need a Diploma in Anatomy &
Physiology or equivalent, and an approved qualification in a
professional bodywork therapy as well. I trained with thermo-
auricular.com.

How can I find a training course?

Find out about the various professional bodies by Googling and
do lots of research. I am a member of Embody
(embodyforyou.com).

What do I need to set up a practice and roughly what will my costs be?

Very difficult to say, but if you don't have space at home then rent
space. Look around your area—you can rent rooms by the hour.
With Hopi it is also easy to treat people at home. The only real

cost is your equipment, which you should have from your course, and the cost of getting business cards and leaflets printed, but you can get these done quite cheaply online.

What is the best way to attract clients?

The best way is always word of mouth, through friends, clients and keeping alert to any opportunity to hand your business card out.

(+0044 7887 661 253; pam@pambennett.com)

Listening

Working in the healing profession, you will most likely find yourself acting as counselor as well as therapist, since you will probably be asking questions about your client's emotional issues in order to help them. Many therapists are natural counselors, as by their very nature they are healing and empathetic people. However, if you wish to hone your skills in this area further to complement your work, you could consider taking a short course in counseling — either as an evening course, or via distance learning through an accredited body.

Cognitive Behavioral Therapy (CBT) can also help you deal with your clients' emotional issues. It looks at how our thoughts affect our actions. For example, the same situation can happen to two people — perhaps an unhappy and unfulfilling marriage has broken down. One person may see the upside of what's happened and think positively and turn the event to their advantage, enjoying time to do what they love, dating and accepting that the relationship is over — while the other person may think 'all is lost' and think negatively, perhaps turning to self-destructive behavior, such as drinking too much, to cope. So with each of these two people, their thoughts will affect how they act. More information can be found at the Royal College of Psychiatrists (rcpsych.ac.uk) and The British Association for Behavioural & Cognitive Psychotherapies (BABCP) (babcp.com).

For America, there is the National Association of Cognitive-Behavioral Therapists (nacbt.org) and in Australia, check out CBT Australia (cbtaustralia.com.au).

A qualification in Neuro-Linguistic Programming (NLP) could also be of use. A therapist using this technique will analyze the relationship between the way their clients think, their language patterns and their behaviors—and how these interactions produce either a negative or positive effect. You study how your client thinks, what they say and what they do and then work towards modifying their behavior for the better. Visit the Association for NLP for more information on courses in the UK (anlp.org), the American Union of NLP (aunlp.org), or NLP Australia (nlpaustralia.com.au).

Chapter 11

Practical and financial advice

There are websites for those in the UK, US and Australia that are an absolute must to check out before you get started creating your new business; all of these are listed in the Useful Contacts section at the end of this chapter. On them you will access a wealth of advice on every topic to do with starting a small business, along with a support team able to help you with any queries you may have, online tools such as business plan and marketing templates and checklists, financial support and search tools to find other avenues of financial support in your area as well as local business advisory services. Again, depending on where you live you may also need a specific permit or license — so check this out before you begin as well.

There isn't space here to cover all the business registration details, laws and ins and outs for each country, so I'd highly recommend checking these websites out before you start: for the UK, visit HM Revenue & Customs (hmrc.gov.uk) and GOV.UK; for the US, visit the IRS (irs.gov) and the U.S. Small Business Administration (SBA) (sba.gov); for Australia, check out the Australian Tax Office (ato.gov.au), Australian Business Register (abr.gov.au) and business.gov.au.

Financial support

For a pre-start-up business in England run by a sole trader (self-employed) there are a few avenues you can explore for financial aid, all of which are listed on gov.org. If you are on income support and a single parent or claiming Jobseeker's Allowance, check out the New Enterprise Allowance. Start-Up Loans, which include mentoring, may be available for those aged between 18 and 30. A Community Development Finance loan could be available for those who have already started their business. Information on financial support in America is in abundance on the U.S. Small Business Administration (SBA) website sba.gov. They offer all sorts of options for financial assistance, including the Small Business Investment Company (SBIC) Program, which can help you out with capital, long-term loans and management assistance if you qualify. Those in Australia should check out business.gov.au.

Another alternative is looking for a private investor. In the UK, head to the Business Finance finder tool at gov.uk/business-finance-support-finder, which will help you to find publically backed finance support. You can also call the Business Link Helpline who will also be able to offer help and advice on any aspect of starting or running a business (+0044 845 600 9006). For America, there are lots of tips and advice on finding and securing a private investor at the SBA website, sba.gov—and in Australia business.gov.au has information on financial assistance you may be eligible for; log on to their website to start your search for grants and assistance.

Alternatively, maybe family or close friends will be happy to lend you money to get you off the ground.

Writing a business plan

With your enthusiasm to get started on your new path, it can be tempting to skip writing a business plan—which can be a very lengthy process. Ultimately though, it is essential, and the more detailed and accurate it is, the higher your chances of success are as a start-up small business. It's a tough environment out there, so you'll want to get the best start you can.

Even if you're not applying for a loan, a business plan will help you because it will force you to make decisions and collate and clarify your ideas. It will also make you think carefully about the direction you're going in and what you will need to get there—most business plans will look three to five years ahead. It can also bring you back down to earth if your aspirations are too lofty for what you have at your disposal, thus avoiding potential failure. You can also look back on your plan regularly once you have got started to help guide you through the start-up process.

A business plan should be carefully researched, backed up with solid facts and figures, and concise:

- Include the name of your business, a mission statement and your unique selling point (USP).
- Include market analysis of your client base: including a customer profile (gender, age range, income, do they already buy a similar service?) and how many potential customers there are.
- State what type of business it is—for example, is it a sole trader or partnership?
- Include an overview and analysis of the competition.
- List the resources and equipment you will require.
- State your short- and long-term business and financial aspirations over a three- or five-year period.
- Include marketing and promotional plans.
- State where you will operate.
- State how much capital you need.
- Include the price of your services, direct costs, projected profits and overheads.

Accounts

Accounting (bookkeeping) is a method of working out the financial stability of your business through recording and analyzing your transactions—your expenses and your income—and it also makes things much easier when you come to fill in your tax return. You'll probably want to hire an accountant, but your responsibility is to keep organized and accurate records by keeping track of revenue via invoices or receipts, keeping track of purchases you make and recording your business expenses.

As Benjamin Franklin famously said, "By failing to prepare, you are preparing to fail." So, keep all of your sales invoices, keep all receipts from your purchases and expenses and keep all your bank statements. You can organize your documents as hard copies in a folder, but if you're recording them electronically using dedicated online software then you will need to scan in both the front and back of receipts—there are lots of online account tools available online to help you bookkeep effectively, such as at sage.co.uk, na.sage.com and intuit.com.au. Whichever method you choose, always keep a backup. For electronic records, take care to back them up on a separate hard drive, USB pen, CD or online using cloud storage—that's online storage space for files, hosted by a third party.

It goes without saying that keeping detailed accounts is extremely important. For example, UK law requires you to keep accurate records through bookkeeping and yearly records for six years. The HMRC can fine you if they find discrepancies or if they deem your records to be insufficient. For detailed information on bookkeeping and other financial necessities and concerns, visit the HMRC website at hmrc.gov.uk, the IRS for the US (irs.gov) and the Australian Tax Office (ato.gov.au) for those in Oz.

Tax reporting

In the UK, as soon as you start your business, notify the HMRC. You can do this by registering your business for taxes online; an online account will then be set up for you. The HMRC will send you a Self Assessment tax return form each year, which once completed is used to calculate how much Income Tax you owe. Essential records that you must keep for your tax return are: records of your sales and takings; records of your purchases and expenses (as a general rule, expenses are for things you purchase with the sole intention of making a profit)—and retain all of your personal and business bank statements.

Keep a detailed and orderly daily and weekly record of your business' incomings and outgoings from the moment your business opens—as well as keeping a record of any other income you receive. If you are also employed, hold on to your P60s and payslips. It's important to keep a separate file for business records and another for personal records. You'll use these to fill in a Self Assessment tax return. As a sole trader you will also need to pay National Insurance—contact the HMRC to find out which National Insurance class your business falls into. It is also worth registering for VAT even if you are not expecting your business to turnover more than the VAT threshold, which is currently set at £77,000.

There's a wealth of wonderful information, including checklists and key dates, on the HMRC website (hmrc.gov.uk) and it's strongly advisable to browse the information on the site before starting up to make sure you know what's required of you. You can also call the Self-Assessment helpline on 0300 200 3310.

In the US, you will probably need to apply online via the IRS (irs.gov) for an Employer Identification Number (EIN)—also known as a Federal Tax Identification Number. Depending on the type of business you are (e.g. sole trader) you will also need to determine which Federal tax obligations you have, for example, whether you need to pay self-employment tax or taxes for employers.

Australians will probably need to register for an Australian Business Number (ABN) via the Australian Business Register (abr.gov.au) and may have to register for a Tax File Number or Pay As You Go withholding and Fringe Benefits Tax—and there are different rules for those working from home. Visit the Australian Taxation Office's website for further information (ato.gov.au).

Top practical tips

- First of all, don't fall behind—keep on top of everything and record things promptly and in an organized manner to save yourself time and confusion in the future. Put aside a set time each week to go through everything to make sure there are no inaccuracies—this way you can track how you're doing and you'll save money when your accountant is able to quickly go through your records without having to correct your mistakes.
- Stay on top of your cash flow by paying your bills as soon as you get them so you know where you stand moneywise, and check your bank statement regularly.
- Record company expenses as soon as you make them, keeping all receipts in an organized folder as proof of purchase so that the tax inspector can clearly see proof of what you've claimed for.
- If you're buying in supplies, review your suppliers regularly and see if you can find a cheaper one—don't simply set up a direct debit and forget about it. By reviewing suppliers regularly you could save yourself money.
- If you become a roaring success from the get go, beware of taking on more work than you have resources to fulfill to avoid running into financial difficulties.
- Open a separate business bank account, which will give you additional tools and protection that you may not have with your personal account, as well as the possibility of guidance and support from business specialists at the bank.
- At the start, it's likely you'll be working alone—but should you take on staff, then you'll need to read up on employment law and familiarize yourself with it.
- If you are working alone as a self-employed person, remember that you don't get paid holidays or time off.

Finding a premises

Unless you're working from home, your premises is likely to be your biggest overhead—so setting up at home, if possible, will greatly reduce your start-up costs and therefore give you a greater chance of success. Alternatively, if you feel comfortable doing so you could travel to your client's home and work as a mobile therapist, which may be the ideal solution as this will not cost you anything (apart from petrol) and you will minimize disruption at your own home if you live with others. Otherwise, you could rent therapy rooms in beauty salons, gyms or leisure centers.

Renting or buying a property are the other two options. Buying a property is very time consuming and it is often much easier and cheaper to rent, which is what most small businesses do as it ties up less capital when you start up. However, you may have to pay a premium on the commercial lease and take responsibility for repairs and maintenance and be forbidden to modify the building—and your rent may be increased annually. Also, be sure you don't commit to a overly long lease—they can run from three to 25 years, which is a long time to spend in a premises that isn't quite right! If you are renting, make sure you know who is responsible for the building insurance—you or the landlord. Health and safety must also be addressed in a rented property— you'll need a fire escape, to make sure your electrical equipment is safe to use and that any gas appliances are safe. You'll also need to provide toilets, drinking water and a comfortable ambient temperature for your clients.

Owning a property has lots of advantages—you can decorate and modify it how you wish, you won't have to worry about your landlord ending the contract and the property may increase in value. So if you have the capital to invest and you can afford it, buying a premises for your business may be the best option for you. However, if you'd like to get a commercial mortgage, you will probably have to raise a deposit at the very least of 15% on top of paying legal fees and other expenses, so you'll need to be sure you're able to afford the monthly repayments.

Whether buying or leasing, always employ a commercial property solicitor to check everything over for you and explain anything you don't understand. Whichever option you choose, finding the best location for your business is paramount as this will determine how much footfall you get. Locating yourself near other similar businesses is actually a good thing, as it fosters healthy competition as each business competes over interested customers. When picking the right spot, consider what public transport links are available and whether there is parking nearby. Consider disability access too, which is particularly important in a healing profession.

Finally, from your research you may have found that there are, say, five people in your local area offering the same service—so if this is the case, consider offering mobile services or setting up your practice further afield. Much more information on finding the right premises can be found at gov.uk.

Sounds good

Finally, if you choose to rent or buy and you wish to play background music, you will need a license—in the UK it's called PRS for Music. To find out more about obtaining this license, visit prsformusic.com or call +0044 845 300 6033. In America, you will need an American Society of Composers, Authors and Publishers license (ascap.com)—while in Australia you will require an Australasian Performing Right Association (APRA) and Australasian Mechanical Copyright Owners Society (AMCOS) license (apra-amcos.com.au).

Advertising rules and regulations

If you're going to advertise or market your business in any way in the UK (as opposed to producing editorial content for a magazine or book) including on your website, you must be aware of the regulations set out by the Advertising Standards Agency (ASA) which are upheld by the Committees of Advertising Practice (CAP). Essentially, you must not make advertising claims that mislead. The UK has some of the tightest advertising regulations in the world.

The easiest way to ensure your advertising copy is up to standards is to log on to cap.org.uk, create an account and then click on 'Advice and Training'. Scroll down and click on 'Bespoke Copy Advice'. This service is free. Here, you can copy and paste your intended advertising copy into the form and an expert from CAP will get back to you within 24 hours to let you know whether it passes regulations. A similar service exists for websites—although this service is not free and typically costs £960. If you wish to use it, on the same page, click on 'Website Audit' to get yours checked over. Getting a ruling for misleading advertising from the ASA can be disastrous—especially if the media pick up on it—so it's really important not to overlook this area of operation.

Before writing your advertising copy and website, you should use the CAP website's excellent search facility to find tailored advertising advice for your therapy. For example, here is an extract from the CAP's advice on Reiki:

> To date, neither CAP nor the ASA has seen evidence to support claims that Reiki can have a physical healing effect on the body. If marketers claim that it does, they should hold robust evidence... In 2011, the ASA upheld a complaint on a marketer's website that Reiki could be effective for a range of conditions such as ADHD, back pain, depression and cancer... Because it was not aware of convincing evidence and the advertiser did not provide any... the ASA told the advertiser to change its website. Marketers should remember that testimonials do not constitute a credible basis for the efficacy of the therapy.

Practitioners of Reiki may make claims for the emotional and spiritual effects of the therapy, their professionalism and therapy surroundings. They may also highlight the relaxing nature of Reiki, its meditative qualities, improvement in a feeling of overall well-being and an improved sense of self.

This is the CAP code's advice on 'healing' therapies:

This is known as and often involves spiritual or religious healing (faith healing), Reiki, psychic healing, intercessory prayer or therapeutic touch. Healers believe that they can act as a conduit for channelling energy to facilitate self-healing in the patient. Practitioners may scan the patient's body with hands, usually without touching it. CAP has not seen evidence that healing has health benefits and claims should go no further than referring to spiritual or emotional healing.

For information on advertising rules and self-regulation in Australia, log on to the Advertising Standards Bureau's website (adstandards.com.au)—and for advertising guidance in the US, visit the Federal Trade Commission (FTC) website at ftc.gov where you'll find online guides.

Wherever you live, the main rule to follow is not to mislead or create deceptive advertising material.

Marketing

Who are your customers?

With an in-depth knowledge of your field, you probably have a clear understanding of who your target audience is—essential knowledge when it comes to advertising and marketing your spiritual business, and equally essential for your business plan. As a very sweeping generalization, the spiritual sector's biggest audience is women, and when it comes to marketing and advertising, you can't appeal to everyone. So, it's important to imagine your average customer and sell to them every time you write a piece of marketing or advertising copy. Think about your average customer: How old is she? What does she do for a living? Does she have children, a husband? How will she find out about your business, and why will she pick you over a competitor?

Keen competition

Knowing who your competitors are and keeping yourself up to date with their activities will help you. Sign up to their newsletters and keep an eye on their websites to see what they're up to. You might spot something that would work well for your own business—and keeping up to date with their prices will allow you to beat them! See what they're changing and what they're offering more or less of. How will you stand out? What do you offer that no other company does? See if there are competitors that are doing poorly and try to work out where they're going wrong. Other research you can do is to talk to business owners—people will often feel flattered to be asked for their advice, so see if you can chat to a few successful business-people and get some tips. On the same note, reading books by entrepreneurs may help you get even more inspired!

Social media

Social media sites such as Facebook, Twitter, LinkedIn and Pinterest are vital to the success of any business in this day and age. It is important to create a profile for your business on Twitter and Facebook, and post updates on these roughly once or twice daily—but don't overload your fans with updates, or they'll start scrolling down, ignoring your post as you are overloading them with information. Consider the time of day you post—many office workers start to get a bit bored around 5–6pm and have a cheeky look on Facebook, or perhaps they check their social media accounts on the bus to work.

By all means use social media to advertise any of your business' special offers or therapies—but you should also use this great opportunity to engage your audience with posts that are unrelated to your business. Try posting inspirational quotes or artwork, sharing links to great websites you've come across, asking people's opinion on a certain subject, asking them to share their healing experiences or even posting a funny picture of a cat or a cute video from YouTube! Engagement with your audience in this way will keep them interested in what you have to say as you are posting fun and interactive things that they'll enjoy, which will keep your business at the forefront of their minds. What's more, if for example you share an inspirational quote, people may 'share' this with their friends, thus advertising your business' Facebook page for you for free.

Send out a monthly newsletter, featuring new therapies or special offers you might have going on. You could also start a blog—this is very simple to do if you have an email account with Google—or there are plenty of other easy-to-use sites to help you get started. Blogging is a great way to share your thoughts and experiences with others. People love reading about other people's lives, the ups, downs and funny bits, so use this medium as another way to engage your potential customers in a way that isn't simply direct advertising. Pinterest is another popular social media site—there, people share beautiful, inspirational and fun images they find on the web. Everything from cakes to artwork— another way to share and engage with your customer base.

Show yourself off

Trade shows and exhibitions are another great outlet where you can advertise your business. The Mind, Body, Spirit Festival in London is an excellent opportunity to showcase your skills and make money, as are MBS shows and events in your locality. Some practitioners won't make too many sales—but more to the point, these events are important for generating leads and enquiries that can be turned into sales at a later date. Many spiritual magazines have pitches at these events, and the editor will take time out to browse the other stalls and pick up business cards and leaflets, so don't miss out!

Creating a website

When looking for a therapist, most people, unless they've had a recommendation from a friend, will head straight to Google and search for a local therapist, browsing through a few websites to check out what each therapist has to offer and comparing prices. Your business details *must* be online, and although you can register your telephone and business on an online directory, potential clients will feel much more comfortable if they can browse a website to see what qualifications you have, which therapies you offer, find out a bit about you and view your prices and any reviews or awards you've received. The option to book online is also very convenient for a customer.

If you lack the skills to create a website yourself, try asking around friends and family first as someone may be a whiz at these things and offer to build you one for free, or at a discount. However, it not difficult to create a good-looking, easy-to-use website yourself—it's reasonably quick and it's cheap, and you can link it to a PayPal business account. Wix.com is excellent and free and you can create a mobile phone website, and a tailored Facebook site, too. I created mine this way in about 4 or 5 hours (charlotteedwards.org). Wix also takes you through setting up Search Engine Optimization (SEO) whereby key words are inserted into your text to help your website appear higher up in search results.

The key to a good website is simplicity. Just in the same way George Orwell said, "Never use a long word where a short one will do", most businesses shouldn't create an overcomplicated, visually confusing website that's flickering with bright colors and patterns when they could create one that places the sole focus on the services on offer. It's inadvisable to write reams and reams of text (unless perhaps on your 'About Me' page, or if you're writing informative articles) as people's attention span online is much, much shorter than if they are reading a book. Potential clients will scan the page swiftly in order to find the information they want. For the website creator, this means short and concise sentences, short and snappy bullet points, lots of white space on the page to make it easier to scan, and clear menu options. Make sure your contact details are easy to find and include your address, directions, public transport links and a map. List both a telephone number and email address, since some people will prefer one to the other.

Lastly, many potential clients will be off put by spelling mistakes or typos, so make sure none creep in. On the same note, if you're going to be offering online courses available around the world it's advisable to use American English spellings of words, e.g. practicing not practising, and favor not favour.

Potential challenges

Isolation

As a therapist starting up a business while potentially also holding down a part-time job, it's quite likely that at times you will feel a little lonely due to the pressures and demands you face. So, find a friend or family member who can support you emotionally and perhaps offer their services if times get tough and you find you have too much on your plate. Also, having a buddy by your side means you've got someone who's impartial and who can offer you sound advice should you need it, and offer a friendly ear should you need to talk a problem through. Let all your family and friends know exactly what pressures you're under and ask them for their support in this busy period. By starting a spiritual business, you'll soon be connecting with many kind and helpful professionals in your field—why not give one of them a call if you need a bit of advice? Another alternative is to partner up with someone with the same aspirations and interests, and go into business together.

Loss of income

Starting a business in the spiritual sector is about wanting to help and heal others—making money isn't a major concern for many people, but if you want to leave your full-time job, or start your business up from scratch full-time, you are going to need to pay the bills. So, bear this in mind. If you don't have savings to support you or a partner who can take the strain as you get going, it is advisable to get a part-time job in the early stages of your start up.

Useful contacts

UK

Barclays (Barclays.co.uk)—provides advice on writing a business plan for a small business.

business.gov.au—all you need to know about starting your own business in Australia.

The Committees of Advertising Practice (CAP) (cap.org.uk)— this organization maintains the advertising codes set out by the Advertising Standards Agency (ASA).

Federation of Small Businesses (fsb.org.uk; +0044 808 20 20 888)—a not-for-profit and non-political pressure group in the UK that campaigns to promote and protect the interests of owners of small businesses and the self-employed.

Gov.uk—the government's website lists absolutely everything you need to know about starting a business. The search facility is great—try typing in 'business' into the search box and you'll get a wealth of official advice.

The Guardian Small Business Network (guardian.co.uk/small-business-network)—inspiration and new ideas for small businesses, also offering events and road shows.

HMRC—to register as self-employed call the HMRC on +0044 845 915 4515 or register online (hmrc.gov.uk). The Self-Assessment helpline is +0044 300 200 3310.

Law Depot (lawdepot.co.uk)—great for those starting out, this online resource helps you to create customized business documents, such as a business plan and confidentiality agreement.

lloydstsbbusiness.com—offers lots of help for new businesses including start-up bank accounts, mentoring and business guides.

smallbusiness.co.uk—this website can help you manage your business' accounts.

America
Federal Trade Commission (FTC) (ftc.gov)—advertising guidance for the US.

Inland Revenue Service (IRS) (irs.gov).

National Federation of Independent Business (nfib.com)—the voice of small businesses in the US.

U.S. Small Business Administration (sba.gov)—a wealth of advice on starting and managing your business.

Australia

Advertising Standards Bureau (adstandards.com.au)—advertising regulations for Australia.

Australian Business Register (abr.gov.au).

Australian Tax Office (ato.gov.au).

Intuit (intuit.com.au)—manage your bookkeeping online.

Other

Google (google.co.uk)—create your own website or blog with one of Google's customizable templates.

Sage (sage.co.uk)—online tools to help you manage your business, including bookkeeping and accounts, planning and forecasting, software for taking payments online or in person and help keeping track of payments and cash flow.

Vistaprint (vistaprint.co.uk)—a website that allows you to produce affordable customized business stationery.

weebly.com—an easy-to-use site to help you create a website.

Wix (wix.com)—free website builder.

Chapter 12

Useful contacts

Akashic Records

Akashic Studies (akashicstudies.com)

Anne Brewer (annebrewer.com)

Slade Roberson (sladeroberson.com)

Soul Realignment (soulrealignment.com)

Susann Taylor Shier (soulmastery.net)

Angelic healing

Angelic Harmony Healing Training Courses (angelharmonichealing.co.uk)—courses in the UK.

Angel Therapy (angeltherapy.com)—run by Doreen Virtue, this site offers Angel Therapy Practitioner courses.

The Diana Cooper School (dianacooperschool.com)—offers highly regarded teacher training courses in working with angels and Angelic Healing.

Guided by Angels (guidedbyangels.info)—online angel workshop.

School of Life Studies (lifestudys.com)—online Angelic Healing course.

Universal Class (universalclass.com)—online Angelic Healing course.

Aromatherapy

American College of Healthcare Sciences (achs.edu)—offers aromatherapy training.

Aromatherapy College of Australia (acoa.com.au)

Aromatherapy Council (UK) (aromatherapycouncil.co.uk)

The Institute of Traditional Herbal Medicine and Aromatherapy (ITHMA) (aromatherapy-studies.com)—aromatherapy courses in London.

The International Aromatherapy and Aromatic Medicine Association (IAAMA) (iaama.org.au)—support and membership for Aromatherapists in Australia and around the world.

The International Federation of Aromatherapists (ifaroma.org)

National Association for Holistic Aromatherapy (naha.org)— offers online aromatherapy training.

TEACH Therapy hands massage (teachtherapy.co.uk)—keep your hands soft with a massage.

Crystal healing

Clear Intentions (clear-intentions.co.uk)—offers a Crystal Therapy course.

Come Alive (come-alive.co.uk)—distance learning course in Crystal Healing.

The Crystal and Healing Federation (CHF) (crystal andhealing.com)—includes a global CHF-registered practitioner list.

Crystal and Healing International (crystalandhealinginternational.co.uk)

Holistic Harmony (holisticharmony.com.au)—courses in Australia.

Institute of Crystal and Gem Therapists (ICGT) (mcscourses .co.uk/xtherapy.html)—courses in crystal therapy.

Natural Energies College (naturalenergies.com.au)—offers a certificate in Crystal Healing.

Vibrational Health Foundation (vibrationalhealingfoundation .co.uk)—a two-year course on crystal energy and healing.

Cognitive Behavioral Therapy (CBT)

CBT Australia (cbtaustralia.com.au)

The British Association for Behavioural & Cognitive Psychotherapies (BABCP) (babcp.com) National Association of Cognitive-Behavioral Therapists (nacbt.org)

Counseling

The Association for NLP—courses on Neuro-Linguistic Programming (anlp.org).

Metanoia—courses in counseling (metanoia.ac.uk).

Open University—courses and degrees in counseling via distance learning (open.ac.uk).

Royal College of Psychiatrists—courses on Cognitive Behavioral Therapy (CBT) (rcpsych.ac.uk).

General

Alternatives—spiritual and personal development talks held in London (alternatives.org.uk).

The American Holistic Health Association (ahha.org).

British Alliance of Healing Associations (britishalliancehealingassociations.com)—join up for access to a range of excellent benefits.

The Complementary and Natural Healthcare Council (cnhc.org.uk)—set up with government funding, registration with this voluntary regulator demonstrates to clients that you meet national standards of practice and are prepared to be held accountable to these.

Complementary Therapists Association (CThA) (ctha.com)—join up for a range of benefits in the UK.

embodyforyou.com—register as a therapist on this searchable database.

Federation of Holistic Therapists (FHT) (fht.org.uk)—join up for a range of benefits in the UK.

Infinity Training Academy (infinitytrainingacademy.co.uk)—offers a range of courses in the UK.

Institute of Holistic Therapies (ihtaustralia.com)—offers courses in a huge range of holistic therapies.

International Institute for Complementary Therapists

(iict.com.au)—offers a range of benefits when you join.

ICS (icslearn.co.uk)—accredited distance learning courses.

The Jewish Association of Spiritual Healers (JASH) (jashhealing.com)—offers spiritual healing.

London College of Spirituality—a spiritual organization in London that also runs events and retreats (londoncollegeofspirituality.co.uk).

National Center for Complementary and Alternative Medicine (nccam.nih.gov).

The NHSTA Directory of Complementary and Alternative Practitioners: a database of alternative and complementary therapists (nhstadirectory.org).

School of Natural Health Sciences (naturalhealthcourses.com)— offers a wide range of distance learning courses.

Spiritual Response Therapy (spiritualresponsetherapy.org.uk)— information and courses on Spiritual Response Therapy.

VTCT (vtct.org.uk)—offers courses in complementary therapies in the UK.

Herbalism

American Herbalists Guild (americanherbalistsguild.com)

European Herbal & Traditional Medicine Practitioners Association (ehtpa.eu)

National Herbalists Association of Australia (nhaa.org.au)

The National Institute of Medical Herbalists (nimh.org.uk)

Hypnotherapy

annejirsch.com—future life progression training.

British Institute of Hypnotherapy and NLP—find a training course (britishinstituteofhypnotherapy-nlp.com).

British Society of Clinical Hypnosis—promotes high standards in hypnotherapy (bsch.org.uk).

General Hypnotherapy Standards Council—maintains high practitioner standards and offers training courses (general-hypnotherapy-register.com).

Hypnova Clinical Hypnosis Training—training in hypnosis (hypnova.co.uk).

London College of Clinical Hypnosis—courses in hypnotherapy (lcch.co.uk).

Past Life Regression Academy (regressionacademy.com)—past life and life between lives regression.

Past Life Therapists Association (pastliferegression.co.uk)— recognizes, supports and promotes Past Life Therapists.

Hopi Ear Candling

Thermo-Auricular Therapy (thermo-auricular.com)—training courses.

Magazines

CADUCEUS
Kindred Spirit
Mosaic
Nova
Paradigm Shift
Prediction
Soul & Spirit
Watkins Mind Body, Spirit

Mediums and Psychics

The American Institute of Parapsychology (parapsychol ogylab.com)—a distance learning training course in parapsychology and psychic studies.

The Psychic Institute of Australia (thepsychicinstitute.com.au)— offers psychic development courses and professional training.

British Astrological & Psychic Society (BAPS) (britishastrologicalandpsychicsociety.co.uk)—offers distance learning courses in a range of subjects.

The College of Psychic Studies (collegeofpsychicstudies.co.uk)—

offers spiritual training courses in London.

Neuro-Linguistic Programming (NLP)

American Union of NLP (aunlp.org)

The Association for NLP (anlp.org)

NLP Australia (nlpaustralia.com.au)

Reflexology

Association of Reflexologist (AoR) (aor.co.uk)

American Reflexology Certification Board (arcb.net)

Australian School of Reflexology (reflexologyaustralia.com)

British Reflexology Association (BRA) (britreflex.co.uk)

International Institute of Reflexology if you're in the UK (reflex-ology-uk.net)

Reflexology Association of America (reflexology-usa.org)

Reflexology Association of Australia (reflexology.org.au)

Reiki

American Reiki Academy (reikiacademy.org) — Reiki classes and certification.

Angelic Intervention (angelic-intervention.co.uk) — workshops on Angelic Reiki.

Australian Reiki Connection (australianreikiconnection .com.au) — a not-for-profit Reiki organization in Australia that offers courses.

International House of Reiki (ihreiki.com) — offers online courses.

The Reiki Association (reikiassociation.org.uk) — a worldwide Reiki community.

Reiki Australia (reikiaustralia.com.au)

Reiki-Meditation.co.uk (reiki-meditation.co.uk) — Reiki training courses in London.

The Reiki School (thereikischool.co.uk) — courses and talks on Reiki in the UK.

UK Reiki Federation (reikifed.co.uk)—offers training and courses in Reiki.

Shamanic Healing

Australian Institute for Shamanic Practitioners (shamanicpractice.com.au)—training courses in Australia.

Foundation for Shamanic Studies (shamanism.org)—training courses in America.

The Sacred Trust (sacredtrust.org)—training courses in the UK.

Second Sight Healing (secondsighthealing.co.uk)—training courses in the UK.

Shamanic Teachers.com (shamanicteachers.com)—find a training course across the world.

Society for Shamanic Practitioners (shamansociety.org)—training courses in America.

"Here is a test to find whether your mission on earth is finished: if you're alive, it isn't." Richard Bach

References

[1] *The Secret*, Rhonda Byrne (Atria Books, 2006)

[2] *The Awakening of Universal Motherhood: An Address Given by Sri Mata Amritanandamayi Devi at the Global Peace Initiative of Women Religious and Spiritual at the Palais des Nations, Geneva, October 7 2002* (Mata Amritanandamayi Mission Trust)

Charlotte Edwards
charlotteanneedwards@gmail.com; charlotteedwards.org

BOOKS

O is a symbol of the world, of oneness and unity. In different cultures it also means the "eye," symbolizing knowledge and insight. We aim to publish books that are accessible, constructive and that challenge accepted opinion, both that of academia and the "moral majority."

Our books are available in all good English language bookstores worldwide. If you don't see the book on the shelves ask the bookstore to order it for you, quoting the ISBN number and title. Alternatively you can order online (all major online retail sites carry our titles) or contact the distributor in the relevant country, listed on the copyright page.

See our website **www.o-books.net** for a full list of over 500 titles, growing by 100 a year.

And tune in to myspiritradio.com for our book review radio show, hosted by June-Elleni Laine, where you can listen to the authors discussing their books.

Printed and bound by CPI Group (UK) Ltd, Croydon, CR0 4YY